CLASSICS FOR TEENAGERS

CLASSICS FOR TEENAGERS

Edited by Shaun McKenna

OBERON BOOKS
LONDON

First published in 1998 in association with The London Academy of
Music and Dramatic Art, by Oberon Books Ltd.
(incorporating Absolute Classics),
521 Caledonian Road, London N7 9RH
Tel: 020 7607 3637/Fax: 020 7607 3629
e-mail: oberon.books@btinternet.com

Reprinted 2001

A catalogue record for this book is available from the British Library.

ISBN 1 84002 023 7

Cover design: Andrzej Klimowski

Typography: Richard Doust

Printed in Great Britain by Antony Rowe Ltd, Reading.

INTRODUCTION

Some young people are put off the idea of performing extracts from classic plays because they think they will be difficult or, worse, boring. But there is a wide range of material dating from before 1914 which is eminently suitable for the teenage performer. This collection of fifty-one solo and duologue scenes aims to bring some of this material to the attention of teachers and students.

The envisaged age-range of the selected material is 13 – 17. This does not mean that all the characters are of that age range – it would be patronising to suggest that young performers can only play characters their own age. Some of the characters included are young, some mature and some middle-aged. What they have in common is that the relationships, the backgrounds and the style are all within reach of the modern teenager – understandable, recognisable and, one hopes, empathetic. Some selections are light, some more serious, some straightforward and some more challenging.

The scenes from non-English plays are given in special translations by Simon Parker, Mary Patrick and Veronica George. Notes will indicate where complete texts of the plays (and other, full translations) can be found. Some of the scenes have been edited for clarity and stageability. Biographical details about the authors have not been included and dates of the plays have not been given – to avoid approaching the material with preconceptions.

As well as scenes that we hope will be fresh and new to you, you will find some familiar authors here – even some familiar plays. In such cases I have avoided the scenes which are usually performed and found equally engaging but less familiar moments. Sometimes I have taken well-known scenes and edited them from a slightly unusual angle.

The book is divided into three sections – Solo Speeches – Female, Solo Speeches – Male and Duologues, the latter containing a range of scenes in all possible male/female combinations. All scenes are suitable for examination, audition and festival purposes and may be used without permission.

For those in search of further material, there are scenes suitable for this age group in the LAMDA/Oberon *Solo Speeches for Women 1800 – 1914, Solo Speeches for Men 1800 – 1914, Scenes for Teenagers* and in the LAMDA *Speeches from the Classics – Female.*

Shaun McKenna
January 1998

CONTENTS

SOLO SPEECHES – FEMALE

SOLO SPEECHES – MALE

DUOLOGUES

SOLO SPEECHES – FEMALE

MIRANDOLINA

by Carlo Goldoni
translated by Simon Parker

MIRANDOLINA is the attractive young hostess of an inn. She is pursued by all manner of wealthy suitors. The MARQUIS OF FOLIPORLI has just said he wants to marry her.

MIRANDOLINA: What a cheek! The high and mighty Marquis of Foliporli wants to marry me, does he? Well, no matter how eager he was there'd be one insuperable obstacle – I wouldn't have him! If I married everyone who asked me I'd have indulged in multiple matrimony. Almost every man who comes to this inn seems to fall in love with me and drips about all over the place. And quite a number propose to me and want to marry me on the spot!

Men who run after me really get on my nerves. I'm not interested in high rank. As for wealth – well, it's nice as far as it goes, I suppose. I like being served, worshipped and adored. It's my little weakness. Come to think of it, it's probably most women's little weakness. But I don't want to get married. I don't need anyone. I live honestly, I'm free and I enjoy myself. I can have fun if I want but I've no intention of falling in love, thank you.

And as for this Knight of Ripafratta! He's about as cultured as a hippopotamus – unbelievably rude! He's the first guest I've ever had who hasn't been pleased to deal with me. What's his problem? Does he hate women? Can he not bear to look at them? Idiot! He hasn't yet met the woman who knows how to *make* him look at her. But he will, he will. (*An idea strikes her.*) Who knows, perhaps he already has! Yes! I bet I could twist him round my little finger if I wanted to. What fun I could have!

Different translations are available in *The Classic Theatre: Volume 1, ed. Eric Bentley (Doubleday 1958)*, *Carlo Goldoni: Three Comedies (OUP 1961)* and *The Venetian Twins & Mirandolina*, translated by Ranjit Bolt (Oberon/Absolute Classics).

TRELAWNEY OF THE 'WELLS'

by Sir Arthur Wing Pinero

AVONIA BUNN is an untidy, tawdrily dressed young woman with 'the airs of a suburban soubrette.' She is a member of the theatrical company of the 'Wells' and here passionately attacks the members of an upper-class family whose son, ARTHUR, has fallen in love with ROSE TRELAWNEY, an actress. An experiment in which the young actress has lived with the aristocratic family has failed and ROSE has returned to the stage.

AVONIA: Look here, Sir Gower… We've met before, if you remember, in Cavendish Square – I spent some of my honeymoon at your house. Just one word about Rose. Now there's nothing to stare at, Sir Gower. If you must look anywhere in particular, look at that poor thing. (*Indicating ROSE.*) A nice predicament you've brought her to!

You've brought her to beggary, amongst you! You've broken her heart; and, what's worse, you've made her genteel. She can't act, since she left your mansion; she can only mope about the stage with her eyes fixed, like a person in a dream – dreaming of him, I suppose, and of what it is to be a lady.

And first she's put upon half-salary; and then, today, she gets the sack – the entire sack, Sir Gower! So there's nothing left her but to starve, or make artificial flowers. Miss Trelawney I'm speaking of. Our Rose! Our Trelawney.

(*To ROSE, breaking down.*) Excuse me for interfering, ducky. (*Retiring, in tears.*) Good day, Sir Gower.

Available in *Pinero: Three Plays* (Methuen).

THE SHOEMAKER'S HOLIDAY

by Thomas Dekker

In this charming and straightforward speech, ROSE is alone in her garden, thinking about her beloved, ROWLAND LACY, the nephew of the Earl of Lincoln. ROSE's father, SIR ROGER OTELEY, is Lord Mayor of London and determined to prevent the match. He has ordered that ROSE be kept within the house and garden. Here, she is making a garland.

ROSE

Here sit thou down upon this flow'ry bed
And make a garland for thy Lacy's head.
These pinks, these roses, and these violets,
These blushing gilliflowers, these marigolds,
The fair embroidery of his coronet,
Carry not half such beauty in their cheeks,
As the fair countenance of my Lacy doth.
O my most unkind father! O my stars,
Why loured you so at my nativity,
To make me love, yet live robbed of my love?
Here as a thief I am imprisonèd
For my dear Lacy's sake within those walls,
Which by my father's cost were builded up
For better purposes; here must I languish
For him that doth as much lament, I know,
Mine absence, as for him I pine in woe.

Available in *Six Plays By Contemporaries of Shakespeare*, edited by C.B. Wheeler (Oxford Paperbacks).

HIS HOUSE IN ORDER

by Sir Arthur Wing Pinero

NINA is a girlish young woman who has always been noted for her modest manner – but her eyes were full of rebellion. She is the second wife of the much older FILMER JESSON, MP, who has been trying to transform her into a replica of his first wife. But the worm has turned. She has refused to assist in the opening of a park dedicated to JESSON's first wife.

NINA: Don't you imagine, any of you, that Filmer can talk me over, lecture me like a naughty child till I'm all tears and obedience. That sort of thing is at an end, believe me. Oh, I know what upsets Filmer so much – why everyone is in such a ferment. Is it because they've a particle of affection for me, because they reckon me one of themselves, that they are disturbed by my refusing to assist at the opening of the park? Not it! Filmer is dejected simply because of the gossip my absence will give rise to – the scandal. There's a screw loose somewhere, people will remark – those who haven't arrived at that conclusion already. And the newspapers! He foresees the nasty innuendo in the newspaper reports! 'The party did not include the present Mrs Filmer Jesson.' ' The charming lady who is now Mrs Filmer Jesson was not upon the platform.'

And you – Lady Ridgely and Sir Daniel – and you, Mr Pryce – and Geraldine – why, you detest me, loathe the sight of me! You are all upset because you are deprived of the gratification of inflicting a grand, crowning humiliation upon me; because you can't drag me to the park and exhibit me to the quizzing crowd, saying to yourselves, 'See! We've brought the failure with us; we have brought with us Mr Filmer Jesson's matrimonial blunder; to do homage to

Annabel Mary Ridgeley that was, whose shoe-strings she is not worthy to have tied.' Oh, thank God I can rob you of that triumph, at least.

Available in a single edition published by Heinemann.

THE PROPOSAL

by Anton Chekhov
translated by Veronica George

This short comedy is a three-hander in which the nervous LOMOV intends to propose to NATALIA CHUBUKOVA. However, he is so tongue-tied that it all goes horribly wrong and he and NATALIA begin to argue about the ownership of a piece of land.

NATALIA: I find all this most upsetting. My father and my great-grandfather both believed their land extended right up to the swamp, so those meadows were ours. How could there be a dispute about that? I don't understand what you are going on about.

Are you trying to make a joke? That's it, isn't it? It's all come as rather a shock. We own a piece of land for almost three hundred years and suddenly it isn't ours at all, we're told. It's outrageous. Oh, I don't care about the meadows – we're only talking about a dozen or so acres, not worth more than three hundred roubles. It's the principle of the thing. I can't stand unfairness. Those meadows are ours! Ours! You can stand there arguing all day, but they're ours, ours, ours. I don't want to take what's yours but I've no intention of losing what's mine, either, thank you very much.

This is all very peculiar. We've always thought of you as a good neighbour, as a friend, even. We lent you our threshing-machine last year, didn't we, and as a result we had to finish our threshing in November. And here you are treating us like gipsies! That's not what I'd call neighbourly. In fact, I'd say it was downright impertinence.

Don't you dare shout at me! Those meadows are mine!

Several versions of *The Proposal* are available, including Michael Frayn's translation – *Chekhov – Plays* (Methuen) and a Penguin *Chekhov – Complete Plays*.

THE WILD DUCK

by Henrik Ibsen
translated by Jean Howell

HEDWIG is a young teenager. Her father has just discovered that HEDWIG is not, in fact, his daughter. His love for HEDWIG and the wild duck that they nurture immediately turns to hate.

HEDWIG: Daddy! Daddy! Don't go away from me. He'll never come back to us again. I think I'm going to die of all this. What have I done to him? Mother, why doesn't Daddy want to see me any more? I think I know what it is. Perhaps I'm not Daddy's real child. And now perhaps he has found it out. I've read about that sort of thing. But I think he might be just as fond of me for all that. Almost more. The wild duck was sent us as a present too, and I'm tremendously fond of that, just the same. The poor wild duck! He can't bear to look at that any more, either. Just think he wanted to wring its neck. I say a prayer for the wild duck every night and ask that it shall be protected from death and everything bad. I taught myself to say my prayers because there was a time when Daddy was ill and had leeches on his neck and said he was lying at death's door. So I said a prayer for him when I'd gone to bed. And I've gone on with it ever since. I thought I'd better put in the wild duck too, because she was so delicate at first. And now you say I should sacrifice the wild duck to prove my love for Daddy. I will try it. I will ask Grandfather to shoot the wild duck for me.

This play is available in many translations, including one by Michael Meyer (Faber), Peter Hall and Inga-Stina Ewbank (Oberon/Absolute Classics) as well as the Penguin Classics version.

TRELAWNEY OF THE 'WELLS'

by Sir Arthur Wing Pinero

ROSE TRELAWNEY is a young actress who has fallen in love, and been proposed to, by ARTHUR, an upper-class young man. She is about to leave the theatre to start a new life. She is speaking to her actor friends.

ROSE: Yes, isn't this a wonderful stroke of fortune for me. Fate, Jenny, that's what it is – Fate. Fate ordains that I shall be a well-to-do fashionable lady, instead of a popular but toiling actress. Mother often used to stare into my face, when I was little, and whisper, 'Rosie, I wonder what is to be your – fate.' Poor mother. I hope she sees.

Oh, Arthur's a dear. Very young, of course – not much more than a year older than me – than I. But he'll grow manly in time and have moustaches, and whiskers out to here, he says. We met because… He saw me act Blanche in *The Pedlar of Marseilles* and fell in love. I always preferred Blanche to Celestine. You see, I got leave to introduce a song where Blanche is waiting for Raphael on the bridge. (*Sings.*) 'Ever of thee I'm fondly dreaming…' It was singing that song that sealed my destiny, Arthur declares. At any rate, the next thing was he began sending bouquets and coming to the stage door. Of course, I never spoke to him, never glanced at him. Poor mother brought me up in that way, not to speak to anybody, nor look. Then Arthur managed to get himself acquainted with the Telfers, and Mrs Telfer presented him to me. Mrs Telfer has kept an eye on me all through. Not that it was necessary, brought up as I was – but she's a kind old soul. And now I'm going to live with his people for a time – on approval. Just to reassure them, as they say. The Gowers have such odd ideas about theatres, and actors and actresses. It'll only be for a little while. I fancy they're prepared to take me.

Available in *Pinero: Three Plays* (Methuen).

CYMBELINE

by William Shakespeare

IMOGEN is the daughter of CYMBELINE, King of Britain. She has secretly married POSTHUMUS LEONATUS and as a result he has been banished. POSTHUMUS is so certain of IMOGEN's love that he enters into a wager with IACHIMO – if IACHIMO can win IMOGEN's favour he shall have a diamond ring that IMOGEN gave POSTHUMUS. IACHIMO is repulsed by IMOGEN but manages to gain admission to her bedchamber at night, where he obtains evidence that convinces POSTHUMUS of her infidelity. IMOGEN knows nothing of this. POSTHUMUS writes two letters, one to IMOGEN asking her to meet him at Milford Haven; the other to PISANIO, his friend, ordering him to kill IMOGEN on the way. IMOGEN has just read her letter and, tremendously excited, is speaking to PISANIO.

IMOGEN

O for a horse with wings! Hear'st thou, Pisanio?
He is at Milford-Haven: read, and tell me
How far 'tis thither. If one of mean affairs
May plod it in a week, why may not I
Glide thither in a day? Then, true Pisanio –
Who long'st, like me, to see thy lord; who long'st –
O, let me bate – but not like me – yet long'st,
But in a fainter kind: – O, not like me!
For mine's beyond beyond: say, and speak thick: –
Love's counsellor should fill the pores of hearing,
To the smothering of the sense – how far it is
To this same blessed Milford: and by the way
Tell me how Wales was made so happy as
To inherit such a haven: but, first of all,
How may we steal from hence: and for the gap
That we shall make in time, from our hence-going

And our return, to excuse: but first, how get hence.
Why should excuse be born or ere begot?
We'll talk of that hereafter. Prithee, speak,
How many score of miles may we well ride
'Twixt hour and hour?

Why, one that rode to's execution, man,
Could never go so slow: I have heard of riding wagers,
Where horses have been nimbler than the sands
That run i' the clock's behalf. But this is foolery:
Go bid my woman feign a sickness, say
She'll home to her father: and provide me presently
A riding-suit, no costlier than would fit
A franklin's housewife. Away I prithee;
Do as I bid thee: there's no more to say.
None is accessible but Milford way.

Available in any *Complete Works* of Shakespeare or individual
edition of *Cymbeline.*

THE TYRANNY OF TEARS

by Charles Haddon Chambers

MISS WOODWARD is the pleasant, plain-spoken and business-like secretary of MR PARBURY. She has attracted the interest of MR GUNNING, a business associate of MR PARBURY. Though he has declared he will never marry, he has become interested in MISS WOODWARD and has asked her about her life.

MISS WOODWARD: I'm the thirteenth daughter of a parson. Why my parents had thirteen daughters, I don't know, but I suppose it is because they are very poor. Two of my sisters run a kindergarten and one other is a governess. Personally, I would rather be a domestic servant. The others remain at home, help in the house, and await husbands. I fear they will wait in vain, because there are so many women in our part of the country and so very few men. I seized an early opportunity to learn shorthand and typing – and – well, here I am. Now you know the story of my life.

Have you ever been poor? I mean being one of fifteen in a family – large inferior joints to last for days – hot, cold, hashed, minced, shepherd's pie – too much potatoes – too much boiled rice – too much bread and dripping – too much weak tea – too much polishing up of things not worth polishing up – too much darning on too little material – and for ever giving thanks out of all proportion to the benefits received. I wish someone would write the history of a hat or a frock – I mean a hat or a frock that has marched steadily and sullenly under various guises through an entire family such as ours, from the mother down to the youngest girl. What might be written of the thoughts that had been thought under such a hat, or of the hearts that had felt under such a frock. Perhaps one day I shall try to write it. In the meantime, you ought to go. You promised, you know. You have nothing more to learn. I don't think in all my life I have talked so much about myself as I have to you, a stranger.

Another opportunity? Not at all likely, Mr Gunning. Good night.

Available in *English Plays of the Nineteenth Century, Volume 3* edited by M.R. Booth (Oxford).

BOX AND COX

by John Maddison Morton

This farce concerns BOX, a journeyman printer, and COX, a journeyman hatter. MRS BOUNCER, a comic lodging-house keeper, has let the same room to both, taking advantage of the fact that BOX is out all night and COX out all day. The action of the play takes place on the day this money-making plan goes wrong. In this extract, COX has just left and MRS BOUNCER, a woman of character, explains to the audience how she makes money.

MRS BOUNCER: He's gone at last! I declare I was all in a tremble for fear Mr Box should come in before Mr Cox went out. Luckily, they've never met yet, and what's more, they're not very likely to do so; for Mr Box is hard at work at a newspaper office all night and doesn't come home till the morning, and Mr Cox is busy making hats all day long, and doesn't come home till night; so that I'm getting double rent for my room and neither of my lodgers are any the wiser for it. It was a capital idea of mine, that it was! But I haven't an instant to lose. First of all, let me put Mr Cox's things out of Mr Box's way.

She takes three hats, COX's dressing gown and slippers, opens door at left and puts them in; then shuts door and locks it.

Now then, to put the key where Mr Cox always finds it.

Puts the key on the ledge of the door.

I really must beg Mr Box not to smoke so much. I was dreadfully puzzled to know what to say when Mr Cox spoke about it. Now then, to make the bed, and don't let me forget that what's the head of the bed for Mr Cox becomes the foot of the bed for Mr Box; people's tastes do differ so. (*Picking up a very thin bolster.*) The idea of Mr Cox presuming to complain of such a bolster as this!

Available in *English Plays of the Nineteenth Century, Volume 3* edited by M.R. Booth (Oxford).

TRUE WOMEN

by Anne Charlotte Leffler Edgren
translated by Veronica George

BERTA is the determined daughter of MR and MRS BARK.
MR BARK is a spendthrift and the independent BERTA has
taken steps to protect her mother's financial future.

BERTA: Oh Mama, I'm so happy – so happy! Sometimes,
you know, a great wave of joy comes over me and
I want to sing, I want to yell at the top of my voice,
I want to dance. I am so happy – but then, I've really
achieved something today. Don't look so amazed. And
don't think, like Wilhelm, that I'm being mercenary.
I've won more than a few bonds today.

You see, it always used to bother me that you cared so
much for Papa that you were prepared to sacrifice Lissi
and me. I remember Lissi having to stop her piano
lessons because we couldn't afford them – just at the
time when Papa was going through a small fortune.
When I wanted to study abroad for a year – that was
very important to me, Mama, and we had already put
the money aside... But no. Papa wanted it, all of a
sudden, so Papa had it. Forgive me for bringing all this
up. I'm not doing it to hurt you, I swear. I realised it
wasn't your fault, you see. Papa had the legal right to
dispose of your fortune however he wanted to – and
you couldn't do a thing. But I still always felt that Papa,
for all his shortcomings, always meant more to you
than Lissi and me – and that you *were* capable of
sacrificing us for him. I hated that, when I knew
I would do anything for you – yes, anything. Now, do
you see why I'm so pleased that I've done what I've
done about those bonds?

Oh Mama, I'm so shallow. Here I am going on about my own happiness when Lissi is sitting next door in tears.

A different translation is available in *Modern Drama by Women 1880s – 1930s*, edited by Katherine Kelly (Routledge).

THE UPHOLSTERER

by Arthur Murphy

The Upholsterer is a short eighteenth-century farce. HARRIET is beloved by BELLMOUR, who is planning their elopement and set out his plans in a letter. HARRIET's maid, TERMAGANT, has inadvertently passed this letter to HARRIET's father, tucked inside a newspaper.

TERMAGANT: Oh my stars and garters! Here's such a piece of work! What shall I do? My poor Miss Harriet! (*She cries.*) Oh, Madam, Madam! Forgive me, my dear Ma'am! I did not do it on purpose – I did not – as I hope for mercy, I did not. I did not intend to give it to him – I would have seen him gibbeted first – I found the letter in your bedchamber – I knew it was the same I delivered to you, and my curiosity did make me peep into it. Says my curiosity, 'Now, Termagant, you may gratify yourself by finding out the contents of that letter which you have such a violent itching for.' My curiosity did say so, and then I own my own respect for you did say to me, 'Hussy, how dare you meddle with what does not belong to you? Keep your distance and let your mistress's secrets alone.' And then, in comes my curiosity again, 'Read it, I tell you, Termagant; a woman of spirit should know everything.' 'Let it alone, you jade,' says my respect, 'it's as much as your place is worth.' 'Who cares about a place with an old bankrupter,' says my curiosity. 'There's more places than one, so read it, I tell you, Termagant.' I did read it! Heaven help me, what could I do? I did read it! I don't go to deny it! I don't I don't, I don't. And then, after I had read it – thinks me – I'll give this to my mistress again and her old bear of a father shall never see it – and so as my

ill stars would have it, as I was giving him a
newspaper, I ran my hand into the lion's mouth.

She bursts out crying.

Available in *Eighteenth Century Drama: Afterpieces*, edited by
Richard W. Bevis (Oxford).

FRIAR BACON AND FRIAR BUNGAY

by Robert Greene

MARGARET is the daughter of a Keeper. She lives at Fressingfield in the country, where there is to be a fair. She has just met LACY, Earl of Lincoln, who is in disguise as a countryman, claiming to be from the nearby town of Beccles. The first part of this speech is an aside, then she speaks to LACY, and to JOAN and THOMAS, two rustic characters.

MARGARET

How different is this farmer from the rest
That ever yet have pleased my wandering sight!
His words are witty, quickened with a smile,
His manner gentle, smelling of the court;
Facile and debonair in all his deeds;
Proportion'd as was Paris when, in grey,
He courted Helen in the vale by Troy.
Great lords have come and pleaded for my love;
Who but the Keeper's lass of Fressingfield?
And yet methinks this farmer's jolly son
Passeth the proudest that hath pleas'd mine eye.
But, Peg, disclose not that thou art in love,
And show as yet no sign of love to him,
Although thou well would'st wish him for thy love:
Keep that to thee till time doth serve thy turn,
To show the grief wherein my heart doth burn.
(*To the others.*) Come, Joan and Thomas, shall we to the
                        fair?

You, Beccles man, will not forsake us now?

Well, if you chance to come to Fressingfield,
Make but a step into the Keeper's lodge,
And such poor fare as woodmen can afford,

Butter and cheese, cream and fat venison,
You shall have store, and welcome therewithal.

Available in *Minor Elizabethan Drama, Volume II*, edited by
Ashley Thorndike (Everyman).

THE BOORS
(*I Rusteghi*)

by Carlo Goldoni
translated by Simon Parker

This comedy about the 'generation gap' is one of Goldoni's funniest plays. At this point the plot has become extremely complicated and FELICE, a middle-class woman, is trying to make things clear in the following explanation.

FELICE: Be quiet and listen! I'll explain everything. No, don't interrupt!

Once you've heard me out, if you still think I've done wrong, I'll let you tell me off. If I've been right, I expect you to accept it. Is that a deal?

But don't lose your temper till I've finished, right?

First of all, my good sirs, the way you treat your women-folk is outrageous! Your wives, your daughters… you are so rough and uncouth… how on earth can you expect them to love you? Oh, they may well obey you – because they have to – but they don't think of you as husbands and fathers but as jailers, tyrants and thugs! Let's just look at the facts, shall we? Signior Lunardo wants to marry off his daughter. He doesn't tell her, he doesn't want her to know anything about it – she's not even allowed to see the young man. She's got to marry him whether she wants to or not. Now, I'm not arguing against arranged marriages – heaven knows where we'd all be if young girls were allowed to choose for themselves – but shouldn't you at least consult her, Signior Lunardo? She's your only daughter! Are you happy to sacrifice her? It's true that the young man is good, he's kind, he's not ugly and he's perfectly likeable. But what if she doesn't like him?

That's why we arranged for them to see each other –
she was worried he might be a tyrannical brute like her
father! Your wife wanted them to see each other, but she
was too scared of you to say so. So we arranged the
business with the masks and I asked the young man to
come. The young people saw one another, and they
liked one another. They were happy. You should be
relieved, not angry.

I acted in good faith. If you are men, you'll approve of
what I did. If you're brutes, you'll just have to accept
I did it. Your daughter is honest, the young man is
blameless and we women have acted honourably. So
send for the lawyer and arrange the marriage.

A different translation is available in *Goldoni: Three Comedies*
(Oxford).

THE BENEFIT OF THE DOUBT

by Sir Arthur Wing Pinero

THEOPHILA FRASER tells her rather colourless husband, ALEXANDER FRASER, how much she dislikes living in Scotland.

THEOPHILA: I understand how you feel. You were born at Locheen. I was born in Chester Terrace. I admit, Locheen is all very well at a certain time of year. But to be stuck there when London's full; when nobody but a poor relation, whose railway ticket you send with the invitation, will come and look you up! Oh, that summer you made me spend there just after we were married. *You* were happy! You were in love. And those pipers! Those pipers! It was great fun for a time but four or five months of Duncan and Hamish and their pipes! To and fro on the terrace, for a whole hour in the morning, those pipes! To and fro, up and down, all round the house, in the afternoon, those pipes! At dinner, from the trout to the banana, those pipes! And then, the notion of your persistently dining in a kilt! A Highland costume on the moors – yes; but in the lamplight – at dinner! Think of it! A man and woman dining tête-à-tête, for months and months; the woman weary, the novelty of her new clothes gradually wearing off; she feeling she was getting lean and plain with it all, salt-cellary about the shoulders, drawn and hideous – and every blessed night, the man in a magnificent evening kilt!

It might have been fun, Alec, if you had the smallest sense of humour; but one soon tires of laughing alone. No, there was never any fun in that kilt. During dinner, not even the table would help me. I declare to goodness I could always see through the thickness of the board and – and see your two knees! Ha!

Available in a single edition, published by Heinemann.

RICHARD III

by William Shakespeare

LADY ANNE's famous speech over the corpse of HENRY VI is a popular choice for teenagers. However, her later scene (Act IV scene i) is equally powerful and is often overlooked. LADY ANNE is with the DUCHESS OF YORK and the widowed QUEEN ELIZABETH, when LORD STANLEY arrives to summon ANNE to Westminster to be crowned the evil RICHARD's Queen.

LADY ANNE

I would to God that the inclusive verge
Of golden metal that must round my brow
Were red-hot steel, to sear me to the brain!
Anointed let me be with deadly venom,
And die, ere men can say 'God save the Queen!'

When he that is my husband now
Came to me, as I followed Henry's corpse,
When scarce the blood was well-wash'd from his hands
Which issued from my other angel husband,
And that dead saint which then I weeping follow'd;
O when, I say, I look'd on Richard's face,
This was my wish: 'Be thou,' quoth I, 'accursed,
For making me, so young, so old a widow!
And when thou wed'st, let sorrow haunt thy bed;
And let thy wife – if any be so mad –
As miserable by the death of thee
As thou hast made me by my dear lord's death!'
Lo, ere I can repeat this curse again,
Even in so short a space, my woman's heart
Grossly grew captive to his honey words,
And proved the subject of my own soul's curse,
Which ever since hath kept my eyes from rest;
For never yet one hour in his bed

Have I enjoy'd the golden dew of sleep,
But have been waken'd by his timorous dreams.
Besides, he hates me for my father, Warwick;
And will, no doubt, shortly be rid of me.

Available in any *Complete Works* of Shakespeare or individual
edition of *Richard III*.

MARIA ARNDT

by Elsa Bernstein
translated by Veronica George

GEMMA is the fifteen-year-old daughter of MARIA ARNDT.
They have recently moved. In this scene, GEMMA comes in
from the garden with her arms full of roses and speaks to her
mother.

GEMMA: Look, Mamma. Roses, dozens of roses. All
from the garden. Right at the back, behind the cave,
there is a real wilderness, our own rose meadow. How
I got stuck! And I tore my dress and I almost didn't get
out of the magic hedge of thorns. If it hadn't been for
the handsome prince – no, he wasn't a prince, actually.
Just the boy from the upstairs apartment, young
Tucher. He helped me. The Tuchers have a son and a
daughter, apparently. They only got home yesterday,
they've been on holiday. Neither of them are educated
at home. She's with the English governesses and he's
with the royal pages. Imagine! So grand!

How are you, Mamma? Did you sleep well? You still
have those dark rings under your eyes. Who have you
been writing to? Have you written to Papa?

Do you mean it? Return to Florence? How can we?
What about your health? What about my studies, my
wonderful lessons? Could we take a professor back
home with us? How did you suddenly decide this? Oh
Mamma, this is so exciting. I wish Papa could have
come here – but, of course, how could he? He
couldn't paint here. No light, no colours and not a
single Botticelli. I've missed all that. Oh, I'll soon our
cathedral and our Giganta and our casa and our
solemn garden of cypress trees. And Papa. Life is
certainly different when there's a man in the house.

You and me and him – we're a family – like Mary Joseph and Jesus. Yes, the Holy Family!

All this has given me an appetite. Shall I ring for tea?

A different translation is available in *Modern Drama by Women, 1880s – 1930*, edited by Katherine Kelly (Routledge).

POLLY HONEYCOMBE

by George Colman

This is a short eighteenth-century farce in which the lively central character, POLLY, has read too many romantic novels and believed all of them! Here, she is talking to her NURSE while awaiting a letter from a suitor.

POLLY: Tell me, tell me all this instant. Did you see him? Did you give him my letter? Did he write? Will he come? Shall I see him? Have you got the answer in your pocket? Have you…? Nay but come, dear Nursee, tell me. What did he say? Give me the letter. What letter? The answer to mine, of course!

He said what? He would send it some time today? Hmmm… I wonder now how he will convey it. Will he squeeze it, as he did the last, into the chicken-house in the garden? Or will he write it in lemon-juice and send it in a book, like blank paper? Or will he throw it into the house, enclosed in an orange? I have not read so many books for nothing. Novels, Nursee, novels! A novel is the only thing to teach a girl life, and the way of the world, and elegant fancies, and love to the end of the chapter. Do you think, Nursee, I should have had such a notion of love so early if I had not read novels? I'll marry Mr Scribble, and not Mr Ledger, whether Papa and Mama choose it or no. I intend to elope.

Yes, run away, to be sure. Why, there's nothing in that, you know. Every girl elopes when her parents are ill-natured and obstinate about marrying her. It was just so with Betsy Thompson, and Sally Wilkins, and Clarinda, and Leonora in *The History of Dick Careless* and Julia in *The Adventures of Tom Ramble* and fifty others – did they not all elope? And so will I, too. I have as much right to elope as they had, for I have as much love and as much spirit as the best of them.

Available in *Eighteenth Century Drama: Afterpieces*, edited by Richard W. Bevis (Oxford).

THE SEAGULL

by Anton Chekhov
translated by Mary Patrick

NINA's famous 'I am a seagull' speech is a popular choice for teenagers. Immediately before that speech, she arrives at the Arkadin house to see KONSTANTIN. Once she was romantically involved with the neurotic young man but was entranced (and eventually seduced) by the glamorous TRIGORIN, a successful writer. Now abandoned by TRIGORIN, she has returned to her parents house across the lake from KONSTANTIN's house. She is emotionally fragile.

NINA: There's someone here! Lock the doors in case someone comes in. Your mother's here, I know. Lock the doors.

Let me look at you… It's nice and warm in here. This used to be the drawing room… Have I changed a great deal? I didn't come before because I thought you'd hate me. I dream about you every night – that you're looking at me but don't recognise me. If only you knew what I've been through. From the day I got back I've been coming here… walking by the lake. I've walked past your house lots of times… but I couldn't pluck up the courage to… Can I sit down? We can sit and talk. Yes, talk. It's so cosy in here, warm and… nice. Listen to that wind. Turgenev says somewhere, 'He's a lucky man who has a roof over his head and a warm corner on a night like this.' I'm the seagull. No, that's not right. What was I talking about? Oh, yes, Turgenev… 'God help all helpless wanderers…'

She starts to sob.

It's alright. I'm alright. I haven't cried in two whole years. Then I went down to the garden last night, to see if our little theatre was still there. It is. Well, you know that. It's been standing there all this time. I cried then, for the first time in two years, and I felt better, a little better… a weight lifting. Look, I've stopped crying, now. Look.

She takes his hand.

So, you've become a writer – you actually did it – and I'm an actress. We've launched ourselves on the world. Imagine. Us. I used to be so full of joy in life, like a little girl… I used to sing as soon as I got out of bed in the morning… I loved you. I had great dreams for the future. And now? First thing in the morning, I'm off to Yeletz. Third class on the train, with all the peasants. I'm contracted in Yeletz for the whole winter season. I expect I'll spend the winter avoiding the attentions of the more educated local businessmen… Life is hard, isn't it. Not what you expect. Why did you say you kissed the ground I walked on?

Several versions of *The Seagull* are available, including Michael Frayn's translation – *Chekhov – Plays* (Methuen) and a Penguin *Chekhov – Complete Plays*.

THE TWO NOBLE KINSMEN

by William Shakespeare and John Fletcher

The noble PALAMON has been imprisoned. The JAILER'S DAUGHTER has fallen in love with him.

JAILER'S DAUGHTER

Why should I love this gentleman? 'Tis odds
He never will affect me: I am base,
My father the mean keeper of this prison,
And he a prince. To marry him is hopeless,
To be his whore is witless. Out upon't,
What pushes are we wenches driven to
When fifteen has once found us! First I saw him;
I, seeing, thought he was a goodly man;
He has as much to please a woman in him –
If he please to bestow it – as ever
These eyes yet look'd on; next, I pitied him
And so would any young wench, o' my conscience,
That ever dream'd, or vow'd her maidenhead
To a young, handsome man; then I lov'd him,
Extremely lov'd him, infinitely lov'd him;
And yet he had a cousin, fair as he too;
But in my heart was Palamon and there,
Lord, what a coil he keeps! To hear him
Sing in the evening, what a heaven it is!
And yet his songs are sad ones. Fairer spoken
Was never gentleman: when I come in
To bring him water in a morning, first
He bows his noble body, then salutes me, thus:
'Fair, gentle maid, good morrow; may thy goodness
Get thee a happy husband.' Once he kiss'd me:
I loved my lips the better ten days after;
Would he would do so ev'ry day! He grieves much,
And me as much to see his misery.

What should I do to make him know I love him?
For I would fain enjoy him. Say I ventur'd
To set him free? What says the law, then? Thus much
For law or kindred! I will do it,
And this night or tomorrow he shall love me.

Available in several editions, including Signet and Edward
Arnold.

LADY WINDERMERE'S FAN

by Oscar Wilde

LADY WINDERMERE is the young wife of a peer of the realm. She has discovered that he has been blackmailed by the mysterious MRS ERLYNNE, a woman with a dubious past. LADY WINDERMERE assumes the worst – that her husband is having an affair with MRS ERLYNNE. In fact, she is LADY WINDERMERE's mother. LADY WINDER-MERE's fury leads her to risk being discovered in LORD DARLINGTON's rooms, which would cause a scandal. Nobly, MRS ERLYNNE takes the blame herself, claiming that a fan left behind by LADY WINDERMERE was actually left by herself. Now LADY WINDERMERE is at home, waiting for her husband to return.

LADY WINDERMERE: How can I tell him? I can't tell him. It would kill me. I wonder what happened when I escaped from that horrible room? Perhaps she told them the real reason for her being there, and the real meaning of that – fatal fan of mine. Oh, if he knows – how can I look him in the face again? He would never forgive me. How securely one thinks one lives – out of reach of temptation, sin, folly. And then, suddenly – Oh! Life is terrible. It rules us, we do not rule it.

She is sure to tell him. I can fancy a person doing a wonderful act of self-sacrifice, doing it spontaneously, recklessly, nobly – and afterwards finding out that it costs too much. Why should she hesitate between her ruin and mine? How strange! I would have publicly disgraced herself in my own house. She accepts public disgrace in the house of another to save me… There is a bitter irony in things, a bitter irony in the way we talk of good and bad women. Oh what a lesson! And what a pity that in life we only get our lessons when they are of no use to us. For even if she does not tell, I must. Oh, the shame of it, the shame of it. To tell it is to live through it all again. Actions are the first tragedy in life, words are the second. Words are perhaps the worst. Words are merciless.

Available in *The Complete Works of Oscar Wilde* (Collins).

SACRED BLOOD

by Zinaida Gippius
translated by Veronica George

This is a dark-toned fairy tale, about a young *rusalka*, or mermaid, and her quest for an immortal soul. It bears some resemblance to Hans Andersen's tale, *The Little Mermaid*. Here, a WITCH is talking to a young *rusalka*.

WITCH: There are humans quite near here. On the other side of the clearing is a little wooden house. Humans live there. Close by it, on a hill, there's a chapel – you'll recognise it by the steeple. Go there tomorrow night – later than this, when it's darker. Make sure the chapel bell is not ringing – that means they are praying and won't be asleep.

Well, don't go if you're frightened. It's up to you. I'm just telling you. There are two humans in the little wooden house – an old one and a young one. Creep in – and make sure they don't see you – and nestle up to the closest one and let him warm you. Just to make sure he breathes on you, touch him. He'll probably wake up and he won't know what is happening. He may start shouting, or chase you, or perhaps even attack you… But you mustn't run away. Whatever he does you must bear it. He will breathe on you and touch you – and you will get a body like humans have, with blood. And then you will be able to see the sun.

No, you won't have an immortal soul, then. Your blood won't be warm, like human's blood, but cold. But you need a human body before you can have a human soul. If you don't look like a human, they won't let you get near them and the Man who shed warm blood won't give you a soul.

Settle down! Stop interrupting! There is much to be done and much for you to learn.

A different translation is available in *Modern Drama by Women, 1880s – 1930s*, edited by Katherine Kelly (Routledge).

SOLO SPEECHES – MALE

THE MANDRAKE

by Niccolo Machiavelli
translated by Simon Parker

The play is set in sixteenth-century Florence. CALLIMACO is an eager young dandy who has recently returned from Paris. He is talking to SIRO, a servant. This comes from the opening scene of the play.

CALLIMACO: You see, Siro, though I was happy enough in Paris, Fate decided I was *too* happy. That's when a certain Camillo Calfucci arrived. He often came to dinner at my house and one evening there was an argument about whether the most beautiful women were to be found in Italy or France. Camillo was arguing for Italian women and another Florentine defended the French. Well, Camillo ended up getting very angry and said that even if Italian women were generally monsters, he had a relative who could redeem her country's reputation all by herself.

My ears pricked up at that. He started telling us about Madonna Lucrezia, the wife of Signor Nicia Calfucci. He spoke about her in such glowing terms that I simply had to see her – so I packed up and came straight back to Florence.

Well, Madonna Lucrezia is even better than his description of her, which is quite a rare phenomenon. And I'm burning with such a desire to make her mine I hardly know what to do with myself. You see, I might need your help. There's a problem. The beautiful Lucrezia is happily married. Even though her husband is quite old – and his looks aren't a patch on mine – she isn't at all interested in having an affair. Not with anyone. Not even with me.

So I'm going to have to worm my way into the family –
become friendly with the husband as well as the wife.
That's where you come in.

A different translation is available in *The Classic Theatre:
Volume 1, ed. Eric Bentley (Doubleday 1958)*.

KING JOHN

by William Shakespeare

This is one of Shakespeare's earliest plays, adapted by him from an earlier work and by no means historically accurate. The wicked King has imprisoned his young nephew, ARTHUR, Duke of Bretagne, and has sent orders to his keeper, HUBERT, that the boy's eyes are to be put out. Here, ARTHUR pleads with HUBERT.

ARTHUR

Must you with hot irons burn out both mine eyes?
And will you?
Have you the heart? When your head did but ache
I knit my handkercher about your brows,
The best I had, a princess wrought it me,
And I did never ask it you again;
And with my hand at midnight held your head,
And like the watchful minutes to the hour,
Still and anon cheer'd up the heavy time,
Saying, 'What lack you?' and 'Where lies your grief?'
Or 'What good love may I perform for you?'
Many a poor man's son would have lain still
And ne'er have spoke a loving word to you;
But you, at your sick service, had a prince.
Nay, you may think my love was crafty love
And call it cunning: do, an if you will,
If heaven be pleas'd that you must use me ill,
Why then you must. Will you put out mine eyes?
These eyes that never did nor never shall
So much as frown on you?

Available in any *Complete Works* of Shakespeare or individual edition of *King John*.

THE SEAGULL

by Anton Chekhov
translated by Veronica George

KONSTANTIN ARKADIN is an intense and angry young man, the son of a successful actress. He despises her 'bourgeois' and complacent success, and holds the wealthy and successful people she gathers around her in contempt. He wants to write great plays which will revolutionise the theatre and has been working on an avant-garde play with NINA, a young girl from across the lake who is in love with him. However, NINA is falling under the spell of a successful writer, TRIGORIN, who is visiting the Arkadins. Seeing this, KONSTANTIN grows increasingly upset. Here, by the lake, KONSTANTIN enters with a gun and carrying a seagull he has killed, which he lays at NINA's feet.

KONSTANTIN: You're alone?

I had the dishonour to kill this seagull today. I'm laying it at your feet. One day soon I shall shoot myself the way I shot the seagull.

No, I'm not the person you used to know. That's because you've changed – you're not the girl I used to know, either. You look at me coldly, as if I'm an embarrassment. It all began that evening when my play failed so miserably. I should have known, of course. Women can't tolerate failure. Well, I burned that play, I tore up every page of it and then I burned it. Oh God, I'm so miserable. It terrifies me, the way you – YOU! – have grown so cold towards me – it's unbelievable – it's as if I woke up one morning and found that this lake had dried up, or soaked away. You can say that you're too simple to understand me but that's nonsense. What is there to understand? Nobody liked my play. As a result, you think I'm an idiot, that the play wasn't any good to start with. You think I'm ordinary – an untalented nobody – someone who's just like everyone else. Oh, I know what you think, what you mean when you look at me like that. I feel as though you've driven a nail into my brain, damn you – and damn me, too, damn my pride, damn it, it's sucking all my life…

Sees TRIGORIN walking with a book.

(*Sneeringly.*) Here comes the man with the real talent, of course. He thinks he's Hamlet – look, he's walking along reading a book, just like Hamlet. (*Mimicking him.*) 'Words, words, words.' As if he's the sun, the centre of the universe… Look at you, Nina! The sun hasn't even reached you and already you're smiling. You looked on me coldly but he only has to appear and you melt. Well, if that's what you want… I won't stand in your way.

Several versions of *The Seagull* are available, including Michael Frayn's translation – *Chekhov – Plays* (Methuen) and a Penguin *Chekhov – Complete Plays.*

THE AREA BELLE

by William Brough and Andrew Halliday

The 'belle' of the title is PENELOPE, a kitchen maid. She has a number of admirers, including TOSSER, a guardsman who has notions of grandeur in his manner of speech. If PENELOPE leaves a pepper-box in the kitchen window it means the lady of the house is at home – and, therefore, TOSSER is not allowed to visit her. Tonight, though, everything has gone wrong.

TOSSER: Alright, alright, no pepper-box tonight – so, in the absence of pepper, we'll take the citadel by storm. (*Looking around.*) Familiar scene of comfort and cold mutton! How oft at that happy fireside have I breathed the hardent vow, and sipped the surreptitious gin and water! In this old chair how many a time has this 'ere son of Mars sat courting of 'is Venus – which her name is Penelope – while the cold pigeon pie has been a-heating up in that there hoven! On such blissful occa-sions, when I have seen Penelope preparing of a tart, how my 'eart has beat at the spectacle of her loveliness; and how my mouth has watered when I seen her a-spoonin' out the jam! Yes – and that commodious cupboard, whose friendly shelter I have so often shared with the black beetles and the blacking bottles, when old Mother Croaker has dropped in on us inopportunely and promiscuously! Where can Penelope be? I am longing to embrace her; and I dined at half past one, which until the present period of evening p.m. is many hours. However, as I know old Mother Croaker ain't at home this evening…

Hears a noise, off.

The devil! She *is* at home; and yet no pepper box in the window gave warning of this untoward circumstance. The old 'uns coming down the stairs. I'll seek the more congenial society of the beetles and the blacking bottles.

He exits into the cupboard.

Available in *English Plays of the Nineteenth Century, Volume 4*, edited by M.R. Booth (Oxford).

THE REVENGER'S TRAGEDY

by Cyril Tourneur

SPURIO is the bastard son of the evil DUKE and, were it not for the circumstances of his birth, would be his father's heir. He is having an affair with the DUCHESS, his stepmother, and plotting with her to get rid of the Duke's heir, LUSSORIOSO. This soliloquy has something in common with Edmund's famous speech, 'Now God stand up for bastards' in *King Lear*.

SPURIO

Duke, thou didst me wrong, and by thy act
Adultery is my nature;
Faith, if the truth were known, I was begot
After some gluttonous dinner, some stirring dish
Was my first father; when deep healths went round,
And ladies, cheeks were painted red with wine,
Their tongues as short and nimble as their heels
Uttering words sweet and thick; and when they rose,
Were merrily dispos'd to fall again.
In such a whisp'ring and withdrawing hour,
When base male-bawds kept sentinel at stair-head
Was I stol'n softly; oh – damnation met
The sin of feasts, drunken adultery.
I feel it swell in me; my revenge is just.
I was begot in impudent wine and lust:
Step-mother, I consent to thy desires,
I love thy mischief well, but I hate thee,
And those three cubs thy sons, wishing confusion,
Death and disgrace may be their epitaphs;
As for my brother, the Duke's only son,
Whose birth is more beholding to report
Than mine, and yet perhaps as falsely sown
(Women must not be trusted with their own),

I'll loose my days upon him, hate all I,
Duke, on thy brow I'll draw my bastardy.
For indeed a bastard by nature should make cuckolds,
because he is the son of a cuckold-maker.

Available in *Jacobean Tragedies,* edited by A.H. Gomme
(Oxford).

BOX AND COX

by John Maddison Morton

For a note on the plot of the play, see page 24.

COX, a journeyman hatter, has unexpectedly been given a day off. He has returned to his room at MRS BOUNCER's lodging house, not knowing that she has also let the room to BOX, who is asleep in the bed.

COX: Well, wonders will never cease! Conscious of being eleven minutes and a half behind time, I was sneaking into the shop in a state of considerable excitement, when my venerable employer, with a smile of extreme benevolence on his aged countenance, said to me – 'Cox, I shan't want you today – you can have a holiday.' Thoughts of 'Gravesend and back – fare One Shilling' instantly suggested themselves, intermingled with 'Greenwich for Fourpence.' Then came the Twopenny Omnibuses and the Halfpenny Boats – in short, I'm quite bewildered! However, I must have my breakfast first – that'll give me time to reflect. I've bought a mutton chop, so I shan't want any dinner.

He puts his chop on the table.

Good gracious! I've forgotten the bread. Holloa, what's this? A roll, I declare. Come, that's lucky. Now, then, to light the fire. Holloa – (*Seeing the matches on the table.*) who presumes to touch my box of lucifers? Why, it's empty! I left one in it – I'll take my oath I did. Heyday! Why, the fire *is* lighted! Where's the gridiron? *On* the fire, I declare. And what's that on it? Bacon? Bacon it is! Well, now, 'pon my life, there's a quiet coolness about Mrs Bouncer's proceedings that's almost amusing. She takes my last lucifer, my coals and my gridiron to cook her breakfast by. No, no, I can't stand this! Come out of that!

Pokes fork into bacon and puts it on a plate on the table; then places his chop on the gridiron, which he puts on the fire.

(*Yawning.*) I'm dashed tired, mind. It would do me no harm to lie down for a minute while my chop is grilling.

He sits down on the bed, feels a lump, turns round and sees the sleeping figure of BOX.

(*Jumping up with a yell.*) Who are you, sir?

Available in *English Plays of the Nineteenth Century, Volume 3* edited by M.R. Booth (Oxford).

HENRY V

by William Shakespeare

Everyone is familiar with the great verse speeches in this popular play. However, the final scene in which a tongue-tied young warrior has to speak of love to cement his forthcoming marriage, gives the young actor splendid opportunities for capturing the awkwardness and embarrassment of a young man we have only seen hitherto as utterly 'in charge'. He is speaking to PRINCESS KATHERINE.

HENRY: Now, fie upon my false French! By mine honour, in true English, I love thee, Kate: by which honour I dare not swear thou lovest me; yet my blood begins to flatter me that thou dost, not withstanding the poor and untempering effect of my visage. Now, beshrew my father's ambition! He was thinking of civil wars when he got me: therefore was I created with a stubborn outside, with an aspect of iron, that, when I come to woo ladies, I fright them. But, in faith, Kate, the elder I wax, the better I shall appear: my comfort is that old age, that ill layer up of beauty, can do no more spoil upon my face: thou hast me, if thou hast me, at the worst; and thou shalt wear me, if thou wear me, better and better: and therefore tell me, most fair Katherine, will you have me? Put off your maiden blushes; avouch the thoughts of your heart with the looks of an empress; take me by the hand and say, 'Harry of England, I am thine': which word shall no sooner bless mine ear withal but I will tell thee aloud, 'England is thine, Ireland is thine, France is thine and Henry Plantagenet is thine;' who, though I speak it before his face, if he be not fellow with the best king, thou shalt find the best king of good fellows. Come, your answer in broken music; for thy voice is music and thy English broken; therefore, queen of all, Katherine, break thy mind to me in broken English. Wilt thou have me?

Available in any *Complete Works* of Shakespeare or individual edition of *Henry V*.

THE SPANISH TRAGEDY

by Thomas Kyd

The BOY is the servant of LORENZO, son of the DUKE OF
CASTILE. LORENZO has used his sister's servant,
PEDRINGANO, to do some of his dirty work. Now
PEDRINGANO is facing execution and has been promised
his freedom. However, as the BOY discovers in this scene,
PEDRINGANO has been double-crossed.

BOY: My master hath forbidden me to look in this box;
    and, by my troth, 'tis likely, if he had not warned me,
    I should not have had so much idle-time as to think of
    doing so; for we men, in our minority, are like women
    in our uncertainty; what we are most forbidden, we
    will soonest attempt. So I now.

He looks inside the box.

By my bare honesty, here's nothing but the bare empty
box! Were it not a sin against secrecy, I would say it
were a piece of gentlemanlike knavery. I must go to
Pedringano, and tell him his pardon is in this box; nay,
I would have sworn it if I had not seen the contrary.
I cannot choose but smile to think how the villain will
flout the gallows, scorn the audience, and descant on the
hangman, and all presuming on his pardon from hence.
Will it not be an odd jest for me to stand and grace
every jest he makes, pointing my finger at this box, as
who would say, 'Mock on, here's thy warrant.' Is it not a
scurvy jest that a man should jest himself to death. Alas,
poor Pedringano, I am in a sort sorry for thee – but if
I should be hanged with thee, I cannot weep.

There are several editions of this play, including *Minor
Elizabethan Drama, Volume 1, Pre-Shakespearian Tragedies*
(Everyman).

ENGAGED (1877)

by Sir William Schwenk Gilbert

CHEVIOT HILL is a wealthy young man with a serious affliction – he falls in love with every attractive young woman he meets. Here, on a visit to Gretna Green, he has fallen for MAGGIE, a local girl, and is horrified when he sees her beloved, ANGUS, kissing her.

CHEVIOT: Pardon me, I cannot allow that! I love that girl madly – passionately – and I cannot possibly allow you to do that. Not before my eyes, I beg. You simply torture me. Angus, listen to me. You love this girl? Then reflect how you are standing in the way of her prosperity. I am a rich man. I have money, position and education. I am a much more intellectual and generally agreeable companion for her than you can ever hope to be. I am full of anecdote, and all my anecdotes are in the best possible taste. I will tell you some of them one of these days and you can judge for yourself. Maggie, if she married me, would live in a nice house in a good square. She would have wine – occasionally. She would be kept beautifully clean. Now, if you really love this girl almost as well as you love yourself, are you doing wisely or kindly in standing in the way of her getting all these good things? As to compensation – why, I've had heavy expenses of late – but if – yes, if thirty shillings –

Now, I'll not have it! Understand me, I'll not have it. It's simple agony to me. Angus, I respect your indignation, but you are too hasty. I do not offer to buy your treasure for money. You love her; it will naturally cause you pain to part with her, and I prescribe thirty shillings not as a cure but as… as a temporary solace. If thirty shillings is not enough, why, I don't mind making it two pounds.

Available in *English Plays of the Nineteenth Century, Volume 3*, edited by M.R. Booth (Oxford).

THE KNIGHT OF THE BURNING PESTLE

by Francis Beaumont and John Fletcher

RALPH, an apprentice grocer, is so moved by reading tales of adventurous knights and damsels in distress, that he decides to become one himself.

RALPH: Certainly those knights are to be commended who, neglecting their possessions, wander with a squire and a dwarf through the deserts to relieve fair ladies. There are no such courteous and fair well-spoken knights in this age. What brave spirit could be content to sit in his shop in a blue apron that might pursue feats of arms and, through his noble achievements, procure a famous history to be written of his heroic prowess? Why should not I, then, pursue this course, both for the credit of myself and our company of grocers? For amongst all the worthy books of achievements, I do not call to mind that I yet read of a grocer-errant. I will be the said knight – my elder 'prentice Tim shall be my trusty squire, and little George my dwarf. Hence, my blue apron! Yet, in remembrance of my former trade, upon my shield shall be portrayed a burning pestle, and I will be called the Knight of the Burning Pestle. (*Calling.*) Tim!

Tim, my beloved squire, and George my dwarf, I charge you that from henceforth you never call me by any other name but 'the right courteous and valiant Knight of the Burning Pestle' and that you never call any female by the name of a woman or wench but 'fair lady', if she have her desires. If not, 'distressed damsel.' Now, shut up shop. No more my 'prentices but my trusty squire and dwarf. I must bespeak my shield!

Available in *Six Plays By Contemporaries of Shakespeare*, edited by C.B. Wheeler (Oxford).

THE MERRY WIVES OF WINDSOR

by William Shakespeare

ANNE PAGE, daughter of a good burgher of Windsor, is being wooed by three suitors but loves only one – FENTON, an ardent and good-looking young man. FENTON has a plan to ensure their marriage which he here explains to the HOST of the Garter Inn.

FENTON

From time to time I have acquainted you
With the dear love I bear to fair Anne Page;
Who mutually hath answer'd my affection,
So far forth as herself might be her chooser,
Even to my wish: I have a letter from her
Of such contents that you will wonder at...
Hark, good mine host,
Tonight at Herne's oak, just 'twixt twelve and one,
Must my sweet Nan present the Fairy Queen;
The purpose why, is here: in which disguise,
While other jests are something rank on foot,
Her father hath commanded her to slip
Away with Slender, and with him at Eton
Immediately to marry: she hath consented:
Now, sir,
Her mother, ever strong against that match
And firm for Doctor Caius, hath appointed
That he shall likewise shuffle her away,
While other sports are tasking of their minds,
And at the deanery, where a priest attends,
Straight marry her: to this her mother's plot
She seemingly obedient likewise hath
Made promise to the doctor. Now thus it rests:
Her father means she shall be all in white;
And in that habit, when Slender sees his time
To take her by the hand and bid her go,

She shall go with him: her mother hath intended,
The better to denote her to the doctor –
For they must all be mask'd and vizarded –
That quaint in green she shall be loose enrob'd,
With ribbons pendent, flaring 'bout her head;
And when the doctor spies his vantage ripe,
To pinch her by the hand, and, on that token,
The maid hath given consent to go with him.
Which means she to deceive, father or mother?
Both, my good host, to go along with me.
And here it rests – that you'll procure the vicar
To stay for me at church 'twixt twelve and one.
And, in the lawful name of marrying,
To give out hearts united ceremony.
So shall I evermore be bound to thee;
Besides, I'll make a present recompense.

Available in any *Complete Works* of Shakespeare or individual
edition of *Henry V.*

VERA, or THE NIHILISTS

by Oscar Wilde

ALEXIS, a young Nihilist, has become Czar of Russia and here sets about banishing the ministers who have contributed to an unjust regime.

CZAR: Traitors! There would be no bad kings in the world if there were no bad ministers like you. It is men such as you who wreck mighty empires on the rock of their own greatness. Our mother, Russia, hath no need of such unnatural sons. You can make no atonement now; it is too late for that. The grave cannot give back your dead nor the gibbet your martyrs, but I shall be more merciful to you. I give you your lives! That is the curse I would lay on you. But if there is a man of you found in Moscow by tomorrow night, your heads will be off your shoulders.

I banish you all from Russia. Your estates are confiscated to the people. You may carry your titles with you. Reforms in Russia, Baron, always end in a farce. You will have a good opportunity, Prince Petrovitch, of practising self-denial, that excellent virtue! So, Baron, you think a parliament in Russia would merely be a place for brawling? I will see that the reports of each sessions are sent to you regularly. You will have time for such literature now.

Bon voyages, messieurs. If you value your lives you will catch the first train for Paris.

Available in *The Complete Works of Oscar Wilde* (Collins).

THE SCHOOL FOR WIVES

by Molière
translated by Mary Patrick

HORACE is a handsome young man, in love with AGNES, the young ward of an elderly man, ARNOLPHE. ARNOLPHE intends to marry AGNES and has disguised himself as MONSIEUR DE LA SOUCHE in order to test the girl's fidelity. Here, HORACE reports on his progress with AGNES to the disguised ARNOLPHE.

HORACE: What luck to find you here! I've just had a pretty close shave, I can tell you. Not long after I left you, who should I see on her shady balcony but the beautiful Agnes. She signalled me to wait and managed to creep downstairs to open the garden gate. I followed her up to her room – no sooner had we got there than we heard a noise on the stairs. It was her guardian! Well, thank heaven for wardrobes, that's all I can say. It was pretty full, mind, with all her dresses, so I wasn't able to see the old man. I could hear him, though, huffing and puffing, getting angrier and angrier. He even kicked her little dog, the brute, and broke two vases on the mantelpiece. The old goat obviously suspects her – but she didn't say a word, bless her, and as soon as he'd stomped off I came out of the wardrobe.

Obviously, it wasn't safe for me to stay – the sad old duffer was still in the house – so I slipped out of the window. But not before we made a plan. Tonight, late, when the old fool has gone to sleep, I'm to hide in the garden and cough three times. She'll open the window and with the aid of a ladder, which she'll hide in the garden beforehand, I shall reach my love's room and her sweet kisses.

I'm telling you this because I know I can trust you.
Besides, I know how pleased you'll be for me. And I'm
so happy, I have to talk to someone or my heart will
burst. I'd best be off. I have to get ready.

A number of different translations of this play are available,
some in verse, including *Molière: Five Plays* (Methuen) and .
Ranjit Bolt's celebrated translation (Oberon Classics).

DUOLOGUES

MISS IN HER TEENS

by David Garrick

This short farce concerns the romantic misadventures of a young heiress. BIDDY is in love with RHODOPHIL and finds herself in a dilemma, which she explains in this scene to her maid, TAG.

BIDDY: How unfortunate a poor girl am I, I dare not tell my secrets to anybody, and if I don't I'm undone. Heigho! (*Sighs.*) Pray, Tag, is my aunt gone to her lawyer about me? Heigho!

TAG: What's that sigh for, my dear young mistress?

BIDDY: I did not sigh, not I. (*She sighs.*)

TAG: Never gulp 'em down, they are the worst thing you could swallow. There's something in that little heart of yours that swells it and puffs it and will burst it at last if you don't give vent.

BIDDY: What would you have me tell you? (*She sighs.*)

TAG: Come, come, you are afraid I'll betray you, but you might as well speak. I may do you some service you little think of.

BIDDY: It is not in your power, Tag, to give me what I want. (*She sighs.*)

TAG: Not directly, perhaps, but I may be the means of helping you to it – as, for example, if you should not like to marry the old man your aunt designs for you, one might find a way to break –

BIDDY: His neck, Tag?

TAG: Or the match. Either will do.

BIDDY: I don't care which, indeed, so I am rid of him. I don't think I'm fit to be married.

TAG: To him, you mean. You have no objection to marriage, but to the man, and I applaud you for it. But come, courage, Miss, never keep it in; out with it all.

BIDDY: If you ask me any questions, I'll answer them, but I can't tell you anything myself – I shall blush if I do.

TAG: Well then, in the first place, pray tell me, Miss Biddy Bellair, if you don't like someone better than old Sir Simon Loveit?

BIDDY: Heigho!

TAG: What's 'Heigho', Miss?

BIDDY: When I say 'Heigho' it means 'yes.'

TAG: Very well: and is this someone a young, handsome fellow?

BIDDY: Heigho!

TAG: And if you were once his you'd be as happy as the rest of us?

BIDDY: Heigho!

TAG: So far, so good. Since I have got you to wet your feet, best plunge your head in the water and the pain will be over.

BIDDY: There – then. (*A long sigh.*) Now, help me out, Tag, as fast as you can.

TAG: When did you last hear from your gallant?

BIDDY: Never since he went in the Army.

TAG: How so?

BIDDY: I was afraid the letters would fall into my aunt's hands, so I would not let him write to me; but I had a better reason then.

TAG: Let's hear that, too.

BIDDY: Well, I thought if I should write to him and promise to love him and nobody else, and should afterwards change my mind, he might think I was inconstant and call me a coquette.

TAG: What a simple innocent you are. And have you changed your mind, Miss?

BIDDY: No, indeed, Tag. I love him the best of any of them.

TAG: Of any of 'em! Why, have you any more?

BIDDY: Pray, don't ask me. When I parted with him, I grew melancholy; so, in order to divert me, I have let two others court me till he returns again.

TAG: Two others? Is that all, Miss?

BIDDY: One of them is a fine blustering man, and is called Captain Flash; he is always talking of fighting and wars. He thinks he's sure of me, but I shall balk him. You shall see him this afternoon for I have given him leave to come while my aunt is taking her afternoon nap.

TAG: And the other?

BIDDY: Quite another sort of man. He speaks like a lady for all the world and wears nice white gloves and tells me what ribbons become my complexion, where to stick my patches, who is the best milliner, where they sell the best tea and which is the best wash for my face; whenever I speak he pats me – so – and cries, 'The devil take me, Miss Biddy, but you'll be my perdition.' Ha, ha, ha!

TAG: Oh, the pretty creature. And what do you call him, pray?

BIDDY: His name's Fribble; you shall see him too, for by mistake I appointed them at the same time. You must help me out with them.

TAG: And suppose your favourite should come too?

BIDDY: I should not care what became of the others.

TAG: What's his name?

BIDDY: It begins with an R – H – O –

TAG: I'll be hanged if it's not Rhodophil.

BIDDY: I am frightened at you! You are a witch, Tag.

TAG: I can tell your fortune, too. Look me in the face. The gentleman you love most in the world will be at our house this afternoon; he arrived from the Army this morning and dies till he sees you.

BIDDY: Is he come? Tag, don't joke with me.

TAG: Not to keep you longer in suspense, the servant of your beloved, by some unaccountable fate or other, is *my* lord and master; he has just been with me, and told me of his master's arrival and impatience…

BIDDY: Oh, my dear, dear Tag, you have put me out of my wits. I am all over in a flutter – I shall leap out of my skin – I don't know what to do with myself – Is he come, Tag? I am ready to faint – I'd give the world if I had put on my pink and silver dress today!

TAG: I assure you, Miss, you look charmingly.

BIDDY: Do I indeed, though? I'll put a little patch under my left eye and powder my hair immediately.

She exits hurriedly. With a smile, TAG follows.

Available in *Eighteenth Century Drama: Afterpieces*, edited by Richard W. Bevis (Oxford).

NEW MEN AND OLD ACRES

by Tom Taylor and Augustus William Dubourg

The Vavasours are an old family who have lived at Cleve Abbey for generations. Financial ruin now hangs over them but during this scene, LADY VAVASOUR and her daughter LILIAN are unaware of the threat. LADY VAVASOUR is in the morning room as LILIAN enters.

LILIAN: Please, beg pardon for playing truant at breakfast, but I was so floored with the ball.

LADY VAVASOUR: 'Floored,' my love? I suppose you mean fatigued. Do drop that detestable slang.

LILIAN: Oh, but Stannie and Bertie say I'm such fun!

LADY VAVASOUR: Take my opinion before theirs, dear. Men may think slang girls 'such fun' but they seldom see any fun in fast wives. All this is that wretched Bertie's doing. He shan't stay in the house another week.

LILIAN: Oh, but just think, mamma, where he'll go in the Civil Service examination if you tear him away from his coach!

LADY VAVASOUR: His coach?

LILIAN: Me, mamma. I'm grinding him up in history and things. Stewing down hard facts into portable historical soup, suited to Bertie's limited digestion.

LADY VAVASOUR: You are as great a tom-boy as he is a tom-fool! And now, tell me seriously, darling – what sort of a ball had you?

LILIAN: Oh, awfully nice; I mean, very jolly – that is, no end of a crowd. I didn't sit out one dance.

LADY VAVASOUR: You danced only in your own set, I hope.

LILIAN: Oh, of course, mamma – except twice.

LADY VAVASOUR: And that was – ?

LILIAN: With a friend of the Bunters.

LADY VAVASOUR: (*In horror.*) Danced twice with a friend of the Bunters, Lilian? Those odious parvenus – who seem to think society's a show, to be entered by paying at the door. If I hate anyone – I hope I don't – but if I do, it's the Bunters, and the upstart class they belong to. And you actually had the recklessness to dance with one of their set!

LILIAN: Oh, but I assure you, mamma, he was not in their style. Not the least loud in his dress, and I should think he's thirty at least, quite what Bertie calls 'an old fogy'.

LADY VAVASOUR: Lilian!

LILIAN: And then I wasn't at all nice to him, of course. Oh, I snubbed and chaffed him frightfully –

LADY VAVASOUR: Really, Lilian!

LILIAN: And Lady Weston's carriage couldn't get up – and the Bunters offered to set me down –

LADY VAVASOUR: You declined the honour?

LILIAN: (*Apologetically.*) No, I didn't, mamma. Well, you see, I thought I should rather like it – Mrs Bunter is such fun with her old point and her new diamonds, and not an H to her back, mamma! And then Fanny Bunter isn't a half-bad sort; and then, of course, dear ma, I didn't dance more than was necessary, and I –

LADY VAVASOUR: Lilian, I must talk very seriously to you and I hardly know where to begin. Every other word you utter is of the vilest slang. You've danced with some low person of the Bunter's set – you've accepted a seat in the Bunter's carriage –

LILIAN: But I did that partly for the fun of making Mr Brown ride outside.

LADY VAVASOUR: Mr Brown? And pray who is Mr Brown?

LILIAN: He was the partner I told you of.

LADY VAVASOUR: Lilian, this heedlessness of yours at once alarms and distresses me. You never had so much need as now of a proper sense of what you owe to society, to your family, to yourself. Who knows, dear child, but that this first season may land you in a brilliant situation, or a horrible fiasco! I have never, like too many mothers, given you a sentimental view of life. I have tried to prepare you for the world as you will find it. Let me see you reward my maternal care.

LILIAN: Yes, I know. You've told me all this before, mamma.

LADY VAVASOUR: I have never deceived you, my darling. Your papa is not rich.

LILIAN: Oh, if I could fill his dear old pockets!

LADY VAVASOUR: It is indispensable that in marrying you should look to a good establishment. Fortunately, you have always had a mother to guide you. Ah, if I had had that invaluable blessing at your age.

LILIAN: I suppose you wouldn't have married papa?

LADY VAVASOUR: I did not say anything to warrant that, Lilian. But I have lived to see more and more clearly that in our station, fortune is the main, nay, the indispensable requisite for happiness. Without that, nothing can make life pleasant. With that, most things that make life unpleasant can be got over. (*Patting her under the chin.*) Never forget that, darling.

LILIAN: (*Clearly bored.*) I won't, mamma.

LADY VAVASOUR: Dear girl, if only you were a little less heedless.

Available in *English Plays of the Nineteenth Century, Volume 2*, edited by M.R. Booth (Oxford).

THE BOORS
(*I Rusteghi*)

by Carlo Goldoni
translated by Simon Parker

This is the opening scene of the play. LUCIETTA is the daughter of SIGNIOR LUNARDO, a wealthy merchant, and MARGARITA is his second wife and, therefore, LUCIETTA's step-mother. LUNARDO is mean, miserable and tyrannical. As a result, neither young woman is happy. MARGARITA is spinning and LUCIETTA knitting stockings.

LUCIETTA: (*Looking up with a sigh.*) Oh dear.

MARGARITA: What is it, daughter?

LUCIETTA: Carnival will be over soon.

MARGARITA: (*Ironically.*) And we've been having such an exciting time.

LUCIETTA: We haven't seen one single play.

MARGARITA: Are you surprised? Sixteen months I've been married to your father and I don't think he's taken me out once!

LUCIETTA: I so wanted him to marry again. When I was alone here, I felt so sorry for him. I thought, 'He doesn't want to take me out and there's no-one else I could go with. If he were to marry someone nice, I could go out with my step-mother.' Now he's married you and, for all I can see, neither of us have done very well out of it.

MARGARITA: He's a miserable old toad, Lucietta. He doesn't want any fun and he won't let us have any, either. Before I was married I rather enjoyed myself. I was well brought up. My mother liked things just so and I was quick to feel the edge of her tongue if she was displeased with me. But when the time came, we had plenty of fun. We used to go to the theatre two or three times a month – five or six during Carnival. Always good seats, too. She found out where all the best comedies were and whether they were suitable for young ladies, and she went with us. And we went to the Piazza, and once or twice to the Casino and we went to the puppet shows and fortune tellers in the Piazzetta and sometimes to the fair. And we always had company in the house.

LUCIETTA: Oh, don't go on!

MARGARITA: It's not as if I want to be out and about every day, but every now and then…

LUCIETTA: What about me? I never go out. He doesn't even like me going on the balcony for a breath of fresh air in case I see a man. The other day I slipped out for just a moment but that awful woman at the pastrycook's shopped me. He all but beat me.

MARGARITA: If only you knew what a hard time he's given me over you.

LUCIETTA: Why? What have I done?

MARGARITA: At least you'll get married and get out of it. I'm stuck with him.

LUCIETTA: What do you mean? Am I getting married?

MARGARITA: (*Realising she has let something slip.*) I, er… I believe so.

LUCIETTA: When?

MARGARITA: (*Evasive.*) When God wills.

LUCIETTA: Could God will it without me knowing?

MARGARITA: Don't be silly. You'll have to know about it, won't you?

LUCIETTA: Nobody has told me anything.

MARGARITA: They will when the time is right.

LUCIETTA: Something's going on, isn't it? Oh, do tell me.

MARGARITA: I… I can't. Your father doesn't want you to know.

LUCIETTA: But we're friends, aren't we? Oh, tell me!

MARGARITA: No. I promised your father.

LUCIETTA: Just give me a hint, then.

MARGARITA: If he finds out I said anything…

LUCIETTA: He won't find out from me!

MARGARITA: You'll let something slip. You won't be able to help yourself.

LUCIETTA: I swear I shan't.

MARGARITA: No. Get on with your knitting. Haven't you finished that stocking yet?

LUCIETTA: Nearly.

MARGARITA: If he comes home and you haven't finished it, he'll think you've been out on that balcony again.

LUCIETTA: Alright, I'm knitting, I'm knitting. What's he like?

MARGARITA: Who?

LUCIETTA: This young man.

MARGARITA: What young man?

LUCIETTA: My intended.

MARGARITA: I don't know what you're talking about.

LUCIETTA: (*Throwing down her knitting in fury.*) For heaven's sake! Nobody cares about me!

MARGARITA: Mind your manners!

LUCIETTA: Don't speak to me like that. You're not my mother. You're hardly older then me!

MARGARITA: (*Cross.*) Well, of all the… (*Relenting.*) I never used to be like this, you know. It's being married to your father. I'm becoming a beast. I can't help it. Those who live with wolves learn to howl.

They both resume their work.

BOTH: (*Sighing.*) Oh dear!

A different translation is available in *Goldoni: Three Comedies* (Oxford).

HENRY VIII

by William Shakespeare and John Fletcher

This late collaboration by Shakespeare tells the story of KATHERINE OF ARAGON, HENRY's first wife, with considerable sympathy. Her successor, ANNE BOLEYN (or Bullen), plays a relatively small part in the action. In this slightly adapted scene, she is seen at court with an OLD LADY, a fellow lady-in-waiting to the queen. There is fun to be had in deciding how sincere ANNE is in her protestations.

ANNE: Not for that, neither: here's the pang that pinches:
    His highness having lived so long with her, and she
    So good a lady that no tongue could ever
    Pronounce dishonour of her – by my life,
    She never knew harm-doing – O, now, after
    So many courses of the sun enthroned,
    Still growing in a majesty and pomp, the which
    To leave a thousand-fold more bitter than
    'Tis sweet at first to acquire – after this process,
    To give her the avaunt! It is a pity
    Would move a monster.

OLD LADY: Hearts of most hard temper
    Melt and lament for her.

ANNE: O, God's will! Much better
    She ne'er had known pomp: though't be temporal,
    Yet if that quarrel, fortune, do divorce
    It from the bearer, 'tis a sufferance panging
    As soul and body's severing.

OLD LADY: Alas, poor lady,
    She's a stranger now again.

ANNE: So much the more
    Must pity drop upon her. Verily,

I swear, 'tis better to be lowly born,
And range with humble livers in content,
Than to be perk'd up in a glistering grief
And wear a golden sorrow.

OLD LADY: Our content
Is our best having.

ANNE: By my troth and maidenhead,
I would not be a queen.

OLD LADY: Beshrew me, I would,
And venture maidenhead for't; and so would you,
For all this spice of your hypocrisy:
You, that have so fair parts of woman on you,
Have too a woman's heart; which ever yet
Affected eminence, wealth, sovereignty;
Which, to say sooth, are blessings; and which gifts –
Saving your mincing – the capacity
Of your soft cheveril conscience would receive
If you might please to stretch it.

ANNE: Nay, good troth.

OLD LADY: Yes, troth, and troth; you would not be a queen?

ANNE: No, not for all the riches under heaven.

OLD LADY: 'Tis strange; a threepence bawd would hire me,
Old as I am, to queen it: but, I pray you,
What think you of a duchess? Have you limbs
To bear that load of title?

ANNE: No, in truth.

OLD LADY: Then you are weakly made: pluck off a little;
I would not be a young count in your way,
For more than blushing comes to: if your back
Cannot vouchsafe this burden, 'tis too weak
Ever to get a boy.

ANNE: How you do talk!
   I swear again, I would not be a queen
   For all the world.

OLD LADY: In faith, for little England
   You'd venture an emballing: I myself
   Would for Carnarvonshire, although there 'long'd
   No more to the crown but that. But look you here.

Hands ANNE a letter.

   The king's majesty
   Commends his good opinion of you, and
   Does purpose honour to you no less flowing
   Than Marchioness of Pembroke; to which title
   A thousand pound a year, annual support,
   Out of his grace he adds.

ANNE: (*After reading.*)   I do not know
   What kind of obedience I should tender;
   More than my all is nothing: nor my prayers
   Are not words duly hallowed, nor my wishes
   More worth than empty vanities; yet prayers and wishes
   Are all I can return.

OLD LADY: Why, this it is; see, see!
   I have been begging sixteen years in court
   Am yet a courtier beggarly, nor could
   Come pat betwixt too early and too late
   For any suit of pounds; and you, O fate!
   A very fresh fish here – fie, fie, fie upon
   This compell'd fortune! – have your mouth fill'd up
   Before you open it.

ANNE: This is strange to me.

OLD LADY: How tastes it? Is it bitter? Forty pence, no.
   There was a lady once, 'tis an old story,
   That would not be a queen, that would she not,
   For all the mud in Egypt; have you heard it?

ANNE: Come, you are pleasant.

OLD LADY: With your theme, I could
O'ermount the lark. The Marchioness of Pembroke!
A thousand pounds a year for pure respect!
No other obligation! By my life,
That promises more thousands: honour's train
Is longer than his foreskirt. By this time
I know your back will bear a duchess: say,
Are you not stronger than you were?

ANNE: Good lady,
Make yourself mirth with your particular fancy,
And leave me out of it. Would I had no being,
If this salute my blood a jot: it faints me,
To think what follows.
The queen is comfortless, and we forgetful
In our long absence: pray, do not deliver
What here you've heard to her.

OLD LADY: What do you think me?

They exit.

Available in any *Complete Works* of Shakespeare or individual
edition of *Henry VIII.*

THE CLANDESTINE MARRIAGE

by George Colman and David Garrick

FANNY has secretly married MR LOVEWELL, against her father's wishes. This scene between FANNY and her maid, BETTY, opens the play.

BETTY: (*Running in.*) Ma'am! Miss Fanny! Ma'am!

FANNY: What's the matter? Betty!

BETTY: Oh la, ma'am, as sure as I'm alive, here is your husband –

FANNY: Hush! My dear Betty! if anybody in the house should hear you, I am ruined.

BETTY: Mercy on me, it has frightened me to such a degree, that my heart is come up into my mouth. But, as I was saying, ma'am, here's that dear, sweet –

FANNY: Have a care, Betty!

BETTY: Lord, I'm bewitched, I think. But, as I was a-saying, ma'am, here's Mr Lovewell just come from London.

FANNY: Indeed.

BETTY: Yes, indeed and indeed, ma'am, he is. I saw him crossing the courtyard in his boots.

FANNY: I am glad to hear it. But pray now, my dear Betty, be cautious. Don't mention that word again, on any account. You know we have agreed never to drop any expressions of that sort for fear of an accident.

BETTY: Dear ma'am, you may depend upon me. There is not a more trustier creature on the face of the earth than I am. Though I say it, I am as secret as the grave – and if it's never told till I tell it, it may remain untold till Doomsday.

FANNY: I know you are faithful – but in our circumstances we cannot be too careful.

BETTY: Very true, ma'am – and yet I vow and protest there's more plague than pleasure with a secret; especially if a body mayn't mention it to four or five of one's particular acquaintance.

FANNY: Do but keep this secret a little while longer and then I hope you may mention it to anybody. Mr Lovewell will acquaint the family with the nature of our situation as soon as possible.

BETTY: The sooner the better, I believe: for if he does not tell it there's a little tell-tale I know of will come and tell it for him.

FANNY: (*Blushing.*) Fie, Betty!

BETTY: Ah, you may well blush! But you're not so sick, and so pale, and so wan and so many qualms for nothing.

FANNY: Have done! I shall be quite angry with you!

BETTY: Angry? Bless the dear puppet. I am sure I shall love it as much as if it were my own. I meant no harm, heaven knows.

FANNY: Well, say no more of this – it makes me uneasy. All I have to ask of you is to be faithful and secret, and not to reveal this matter till we disclose it to the family ourselves.

BETTY: If I say a word, I wish I may be burned. And as for Mr Lovewell, I am sure I have loved the dear gentleman ever since he got a tide-waiter's place for my brother. But let me tell you both, you must leave off your soft looks to each others, and your whispers, and your glances, and your always sitting next to one another at dinner, and your long walks together in the evening. For my part, if I had not been in on the secret, I would have known you were a pair of lovers at least, if not man and wife, as –

FANNY: Sssh! See now there, again. Pray be careful.

BETTY: Well, well. Nobody hears me! Hark! I hear your husband. I'll slip down the back stairs and leave you together.

She exits.

FANNY: I see, I see I shall never have a moment's ease till our marriage is made public. New distresses crowd in upon me every day. The solicitude of my mind sinks my spirits, preys upon my health, and destroys every comfort of my life. It shall be revealed, no matter what the consequence!

Available in *Plays of The Eighteenth Century* (Everyman).

HER SOUL

by Amelia Rosselli
translated by Mary Patrick

OLGA is a painter and MARIETTA her model. MARIETTA is posing for a portrait. This scene opens the play.

OLGA: (*Impatiently.*) Hold your head up! More to the right… that's enough. Back a little. That's it. And do try to stay still. (*Painting, then…*) It's no good. What's the matter with you today? I can't do anything with you like this. You'd better go home. This is a waste of time.

MARIETTA starts sobbing.

I've made you cry. I'm sorry. You know how I get when I'm agitated.

MARIETTA: It's not that.

OLGA: What then? Don't you feel well? If you'd told me, we could have stopped earlier.

MARIETTA: He's… he's left me.

OLGA: Leonardi? Left you? He can't have done. Have you been quarrelling again? Well, lovers do quarrel. I expect he's waiting for you at home.

MARIETTA: No, he's gone.

OLGA: Gone?

MARIETTA: He left two days ago. He took all his things. He's not coming back. I know he isn't, I know *him*. If he'd just walked out I'd still hope – he has a terrible temper. But he was so calm, so cold…

OLGA: Did he say why?

MARIETTA: He said… he said that just because things had gone well so far, that didn't mean they would always be alright and he had to think about his own future, and told me to think about mine.

OLGA: That was mean.

MARIETTA: And then… He treated me as if… as if I was a prostitute.

OLGA: Oh you poor thing. But I did warn you about Leonardi.

MARIETTA: I loved him.

OLGA: He only thinks about himself. He stayed with you while it suited him. Now he's become successful and he's mixing in a different circle, he thinks he doesn't need you. And you give him the satisfaction of showing him how upset you are. Have you no pride?

MARIETTA: I don't care about pride. Where will that get me now? Everyone will know. They'll insult me to my face.

OLGA: Just because you lived with him doesn't mean…

MARIETTA: I never meant any harm… I loved him, that was all. If I'd been more cunning I wouldn't still be just a model.

OLGA: Is that such a bad thing to be?

MARIETTA: When I think about our baby… Even if he doesn't care about me, doesn't he care about his son? And what will I say when he asks me about his father? What will I tell him?

OLGA: The truth.

MARIETTA hides her face in her hands.

Don't be ashamed of loving someone you thought was worthy. It would have been far more shameful to have pretended to love him in order to get your own way.

MARIETTA: Thank you for saying that. It does help. I felt that, somewhere inside, but I couldn't find the words.

OLGA: Poor Marietta. We all have that inner voice, you know, but it's hard to listen to it when everyone else is putting their oar in. Now, be brave and remember – I'm always here. Anything you need.

MARIETTA: Thank you, Signorina.

OLGA: You'd better get dressed. I'm expecting guests.

MARIETTA: Do you want me tomorrow?

OLGA: Yes. Can you make it any earlier?

MARIETTA: Certainly.

OLGA: And if there's a problem, I'll send you a note. The usual address?

MARIETTA: No. No, I've had to move out. I'm just going back there to pick up my belongings.

OLGA: Are you moving?

MARIETTA: I can't stay. The rent is only paid up until today.

OLGA: Where will you go?

MARIETTA: God will provide.

OLGA: What about the baby?

MARIETTA: Still with the wet-nurse, thank God.

OLGA: But where will you sleep tonight?

MARIETTA: I'll find… somewhere.

OLGA: Marietta!

MARIETTA: It's alright.

OLGA: It is not alright. You'll come here till you can find a decent room.

MARIETTA: Here?

OLGA: Certainly.

MARIETTA: You're very kind but... I can't. What will people say.

OLGA: I don't care what people say. You can sleep in the room where I keep my canvases. Don't argue, Marietta. It is all arranged. Go and fetch your things.

MARIETTA: I don't know how to thank you, Signorina.

OLGA: Don't bother to thank me. I'll see you later, then.

MARIETTA: Yes. Thank you. Thank you.

A different translation is available in *Modern Drama by Women 1880s – 1930s*, edited by Katherine Kelly (Routledge).

THE SERVANT OF TWO MASTERS

by Carlo Goldoni
translated by Simon Parker

The plot of this play, based on traditional Commedia dell' Arte characters, is too complex to explain briefly. TRUFFALDINO has managed to make his life complicated by serving two masters. Here, SMERALDINA, the maid of a beautiful young woman, CLARICE, comes to the tavern where TRUFFALDINO and his masters are staying. SMERALDINA is attracted to TRUFFALDINO.

TRUFFALDINO: (*Entering with a bottle, glass and napkin in his hand.*) Did someone ask for me?

SMERALDINA: Yes, me. Sorry to trouble you.

TRUFFALDINO: (*Looking her up and down.*) No trouble, I assure you. What can I do for you?

SMERALDINA: I haven't interrupted your dinner, have I?

TRUFFALDINO: No problem. I can go back to it.

SMERALDINA: Oh, I *am* sorry.

TRUFFALDINO: Are you? *I'm* over the moon. The fact is, I've eaten quite enough dinner and your sparkling eyes are just the thing to help me digest it.

SMERALDINA: (*Aside.*) Oh, isn't he charming!

TRUFFALDINO: Just let me put this bottle down, my dear, and I'm all yours.

SMERALDINA: (*Aside.*) He called me 'my dear!'

(*To TRUFFALDINO.*) My mistress sends this letter to Signor Federigo Rasponi. I didn't want to come in to the tavern myself so I thought I'd ask you to deliver it.

TRUFFALDINO: That's easily done. I have a message for you, too.

SMERALDINA: For me? From whom?

TRUFFALDINO: A very honest man, a wonderful man. Tell me, do you know Signor Truffaldino Battochio?

SMERALDINA: I don't think so… (*Aside.*) I bet it's him!

TRUFFALDINO: He's very good-looking. Very. And clever, funny, fit… Oh, he's one in a million.

SMERALDINA: I don't recognise the description.

TRUFFALDINO: You *have* met him, though. And what's more, he's in love with you.

SMERALDINA: Oh! You're teasing me. Stop it.

TRUFFALDINO: If he thought he had a chance, he'd introduce himself.

SMERALDINA: Well… If I were to see him… and if I liked him… perhaps he might have a chance.

TRUFFALDINO: Would you like to see him now?

SMERALDINA: I don't mind if I do.

TRUFFALDINO: Hang on a minute, then.

TRUFFALDINO exits.

SMERALDINA: (*Disappointed.*) Oh! It isn't him.

TRUFFALDINO enters, makes low bows to SMERALDINA, passes close by her, sighs and goes back into the tavern.

What's going on? I don't understand this.

TRUFFALDINO re-enters.

TRUFFALDINO: Did you see him?

SMERALDINA: See who?

TRUFFALDINO: The man who's in love with you.

SMERALDINA: I only saw you.

TRUFFALDINO: (*Sighing.*) Well?

SMERALDINA: So it's you who's in love with me?

TRUFFALDINO: (*Sighing.*) You bet!

SMERALDINA: Why didn't you just say so?

TRUFFALDINO: I'm very shy.

SMERALDINA: (*Aside.*) Oh, who could resist him?

TRUFFALDINO: Well?

SMERALDINA: Well…

TRUFFALDINO: Go on, tell me.

SMERALDINA: I'm rather shy, too.

TRUFFALDINO: Perfect. We can be shy together.

SMERALDINA: (*Laughing.*) You're very silly.

TRUFFALDINO: Mmmm. But I'm free, single and unattached.

SMERALDINA: Me too. Not that I couldn't have been married fifty times over by now, if I'd wanted. I just…

TRUFFALDINO: Never found the right man?

SMERALDINA: No.

TRUFFALDINO: Not until now.

SMERALDINA: That remains to be seen. I… No, I'm not going to say another word..

A different translation is available in *The Classic Theatre: Volume 1, ed. Eric Bentley* (Doubleday).

MACBETH

by William Shakespeare

The DOCTOR and the GENTLEWOMAN, servants of LADY MACBETH, Queen of Scotland, are concerned about her mental state. She has been sleepwalking. The GENTLEWOMAN has summoned the DOCTOR.

DOCTOR: I have two nights watched with you, but can perceive no truth in your report. When was it she last walked?

GENTLEWOMAN: Since his majesty went into the field, I have seen her rise from her bed, throw her nightgown upon her, unlock her closet, take forth paper, fold it, write upon't, read it, afterwards seal it, and again return to bed; yet all this time in a fast sleep.

DOCTOR: A great perturbation in nature, to receive at once the benefit of sleep and do the effects of watching! In this slumbery agitation, besides her walking and other actual performances, what, at any time, have you heard her say?

GENTLEWOMAN: That, sir, which I will not report after her.

DOCTOR: You may to me; and it is most meet you should.

GENTLEWOMAN: Neither to you nor any one, having no witness to confirm my speech.

LADY MACBETH enters, carrying a taper.

Lo you, here she comes. This is her very guise, and, upon my life, fast asleep. Observe her; stand close.

DOCTOR: How came she by that light?

GENTLEWOMAN: Why, it stood by her: she has light by her continually: 'tis her command.

DOCTOR: You see, her eyes are open.

GENTLEWOMAN: Ay, but their sense is shut.

DOCTOR: What is it she does now? Look, how she rubs her hands.

GENTLEWOMAN: It is an accustomed action with her, to seem thus washing her hands: I have known her continue in this a quarter of an hour.

DOCTOR: Hark, she speaks. (*Taking out a book.*) I will set down what comes from her, to satisfy my remembrance the more strongly.

They listen. The DOCTOR makes notes.

Do you mark that?

They listen again.

Go to, go to; you have known what you should not.

GENTLEWOMAN: She has spoke what she should not, I am sure of that; heaven knows what she has known.

DOCTOR: What a sigh is there: the heart is sorely charged.

GENTLEWOMAN: I would not have such a heart in my bosom for the dignity of the whole body.

DOCTOR: Well, well, well.

GENTLEWOMAN: Pray God it be, sir.

DOCTOR: This disease is beyond my practice: yet I have known those which have walked in their sleep who have died holily in their beds. Even so… Will she go now to bed?

GENTLEWOMAN: Directly.

DOCTOR: Foul whisperings are abroad: unnatural deeds
    Do breed unnatural troubles: infected minds

To their deaf pillows will discharge their secrets:
More needs she the divine than the physician.
God, God forgive us all! Look after her;
Remove from her the means of all annoyance,
And still keep eyes upon her. So, goodnight:
My mind she has mated and amazed my sight:
I think, but dare not speak.

GENTLEWOMAN: Good night, good doctor.

Available in any *Complete Works* of Shakespeare or individual edition of *Macbeth*.

QUALITY STREET

by J. M. Barrie

In this romantic comedy, PHOEBE, the pretty young mistress of the house, is ostensibly telling off the RECRUITING SERGEANT for being a follower of her maid. In fact, she is using the opportunity to find out about VALENTINE, whom she loves from a distance. She is aware throughout the scene that people are listening outside the door. Barrie tells us that the SERGEANT is Irish, but another accent might be substituted.

PHOEBE: Sergeant!

SERGEANT: Your sarvint, ma'am. (*He salutes.*)

He drops his hand from the salute – PHOEBE retreats. She is as perplexed as he seems undismayed. She sees mud from his boots on the carpet.

PHOEBE: Oh! Oh – stop!

She gets a paper from the work-table. She opens the paper once, looks at his boots, and opens the paper fuller.

Sergeant, I am wishful to scold you, but would you be so obliging as to stand on this paper while I do it?

SERGEANT: With all the pleasure in life, ma'am.

PHOEBE: (*Spreading paper on floor.*) Lift your feet –

The SERGEANT lifts one foot.

Both of them.

The SERGEANT stands on the paper.

Sergeant, have you – killed people?

SERGEANT: Dozens, ma'am, dozens.

PHOEBE: How terrible! Oh, sir, I pray every night that the Lord in his loving kindness will root the enemy up. Is it true that Napoleon eats babies?

SERGEANT: I have seen him do it, ma'am.

PHOEBE: The man of sin! Oh, Sergeant, a shudder goes through me when I see you in the streets enticing these poor young men.

SERGEANT: If you were one them, ma'am, and death or glory was the call, *you* would take the shilling, ma'am.

PHOEBE: Oh, not for that!

SERGEANT: (*Springing to attention.*) For King and Country, ma'am.

PHOEBE: (*Grandly.*) Yes, yes, for that!

SERGEANT: Not that it's all fighting. The sack of captured towns, the loot –

PHOEBE: (*Proudly.*) An English soldier never sacks or loots.

SERGEANT: (*At attention.*) No, ma'am! And then – the girls.

PHOEBE: What girls?

SERGEANT: In the towns that – we don't sack.

PHOEBE: (*Haughty.*) How they must hate the haughty conqueror.

SERGEANT: We – we are not so haughty as all that. And – oh – of an evening you should see us marching down the street.

He marches with an arm round an imaginary girl.

PHOEBE: But why do you hold your arm out?

SERGEANT: Why ma'am – You see, 'tis a military custom, ma'am, that makes the Irish soldier loved all over the world.

PHOEBE: I think I understand. Oh Sergeant, I fear you do not tell those poor young men the noble things I thought you told them.

SERGEANT: Ma'am, I must tell them what they are wishful to hear. There ha' been five men, all this week, listening to me, and then showing me their heels, but by a grand stroke of luck, I have them at last.

PHOEBE: Luck?

SERGEANT: The luck, ma'am, is that a gentleman of the town has enlisted. That gave 'em a push forward.

PHOEBE: A gentleman of this town enlisted? Sergeant, who?

SERGEANT: Why, ma'am, I think it be a secret as yet.

PHOEBE: But a gentleman! This is the most amazing, exciting thing. Sergeant, be so obliging.

SERGEANT: Nay, ma'am, I can't.

PHOEBE: (*Disappointed.*) Sergeant, I have not been saying the things I meant to say to you. Will you please excuse me turning you out of the house somewhat violently?

SERGEANT: I am used to it, ma'am.

PHOEBE: I won't really hurt you.

SERGEANT: Thank you kindly, ma'am.

> *PHOEBE looks round at the door and assumes a stern expression. The SERGEANT grins through her speech.*

PHOEBE: I protest, sir; we shall permit no followers in this house. Should I discover you in my kitchen again, I shall pitch you out – neck and crop! (*More gently.*) A glass of cowslip wine, sir?

SERGEANT: If not too strong, ma'am.

PHOEBE pours a glass of wine and brings it to the SERGEANT.

Thank you kindly, ma'am.

He takes out a handkerchief and ties it round the stem of the glass.

PHOEBE: Why do you do that, sir?

SERGEANT: I was afraid I might swallow the glass.

He drinks, holding the handkerchief in his left hand. He hands the glass to her.

PHOEBE: How strange!

She hears a noise and looks around, and indicates the presence of the others to the SERGEANT, who smiles and stands to attention. PHOEBE now speaks with all the authority she can muster.

Begone, sir! Begone.

The SERGEANT winks at her, turns on his heels and exits. PHOEBE goes to the other door.

You can come in now. He will not trouble us again.

Available as a single play from Samuel French Ltd. and in some collected editions of Barrie's works.

THE SHOEMAKER'S HOLIDAY

by Thomas Dekker

JANE is the wife of a shoemaker who is away fighting the wars. HAMMON, a London citizen, has taken a fancy to her and here sets out to woo her.

HAMMON: In faith, I love you.

JANE: I believe you do.

HAMMON: Shall a true love in me breed love in you?

JANE: I hate you not.

HAMMON: Then you must love.

JANE: I do.
    What, are you better now? I love not you!

HAMMON: All this, I hope, is but a woman's fray,
    That means, 'come to me' when she cries 'away!'
    In earnest, mistress dear, I do not jest.
    A true chaste love hath entered in my breast.
    I love you dearly, as I love my life –
    I love you as a husband loves a wife;
    That, and no other love, my love requires.
    Thy wealth, I know, is little; my desires
    Thirst not for gold. Sweet, beauteous Jane, what's mine
    Shall, if thou make myself thine, all be thine.

JANE: Good sir, I do believe you love me well;
    For 'tis a silly conquest, silly pride
    For one like you – I mean a gentleman –
    To boast that by his love-tricks he hath brought
    Such and such women to his amorous lure;
    I think you do not so, yet many do,
    And make it even a very trade to woo.
    I could be coy, as many women be,

Feed you with sunshine smiles and wanton looks,
But I detest such witchcraft; say that I
Do constantly believe you, constant have –

HAMMON: Why dost thou not believe me?

JANE: I believe you;
But yet, good sir, because I will not grieve you
With hopes to taste fruit that will never fall,
In simple truth, this is the sum of all:
My husband lives, at least I hope he lives.
Pressed was he to these bitter wars in France;
Bitter they are to me by wanting him.
I have but one heart and that heart's his due.
How can I then bestow the same on you?

HAMMON: Chaste and poor woman, I will not abuse thee,
Although it cost my life if you refuse me.
Thy husband, pressed for France, what was his name?

JANE: Ralph Damport.

HAMMON: Damport? Here's a letter sent
From France to me, from a dear friend of mine,
A gentleman of place; here he doth write
The names that have been slain in every fight.

JANE: I hope death's scroll contains not my love's name.

HAMMON: Cannot you read?

JANE: I can.

HAMMON: Peruse the same.
To my remembrance such a name I read
Amongst the rest. See here.

JANE: Ay me, he's dead!
He's dead! If this be true, my dear heart's slain!

HAMMON: Have patience, dear love.

JANE: Hence, hence!

HAMMON: Nay, sweet Jane,
    Make not poor sorrow proud with these rich tears.
    I mourn thy husband's death because thou mourn'st.

JANE: That bill is forg'd: 'tis signed by forgery!

HAMMON: I'll bring thee letters sent besides to many,
    Carrying the like report: Jane, 'tis too true.
    Come, weep not: mourning, though it rise from love,
    Helps not the mournèd, yet hurts them that mourn.

JANE: For God's sake, leave me.

HAMMON: Whither dost thou turn?
    Forget the dead, love them that are alive;
    His love is jaded: try how mine will thrive.

JANE: 'Tis now no time for me to think on love.

HAMMON: 'Tis now best time for you to think on love,
    Because your love lives not.

JANE: Though he be dead,
    My love to him shall not be burièd;
    For God's sake, leave me to myself alone.

HAMMON: Answer me to my suit and I am gone.
    Say to me yea or nay!

JANE: For God's love, peace!
    My sorrows by your presence more increase.
    Thus much I say, and saying bid adieu,
    If ever I love man, it shall be you.

HAMMON: Oh, blessed voice! Dear Jane, I'll urge no more,
    Thy breath hath made me rich.

JANE: Death makes me poor.

Available in *Six Plays By Contemporaries of Shakespeare*, edited by C.B. Wheeler (Oxford).

THE FAN
(*Il Ventaglio*)

by Carlo Goldoni
translated by Simon Parker

The COUNT is not as important a figure in the village as he likes to believe. He has been asked to speak to GIANNINA, a pert country girl, by her brother, who has a husband in mind for her. GIANNINA has her own ideas.

COUNT: There she is! Here, girl, here!

GIANNINA: Sir?

COUNT: Just a quick word.

GIANNINA: It's rather a nuisance.

COUNT: Where are you going?

GIANNINA: None of your business.

COUNT: How dare you speak to me like that!

GIANNINA: I speak the only way I know and I speak the same to everyone.

COUNT: Don't you know who I am? How important I am?

GIANNINA: Look, did you want something or are you talking for the sake of it? Your Honour.

COUNT: Your Excellency, actually.

GIANNINA: (*Aside.*) Your Stuck Up Your Own Bottom-ness, more like.

COUNT: Come here.

GIANNINA: I am here.

COUNT: Do you want to get married?

GIANNINA: Yes.

COUNT: Oh, good girl.

GIANNINA: What goes round in my head comes out through my mouth.

COUNT: Would you like me to find you a husband?

GIANNINA: No.

COUNT: No? Why not?

GIANNINA: I can find one on my own, thank you.

COUNT: But you could pick a wrong 'un. I could protect you.

GIANNINA: No, thanks.

COUNT: You know how powerful I am round here.

GIANNINA: Not when it comes to my love life, you're not.

COUNT: You're in love with Crespino.

GIANNINA: (*Evasive.*) He's alright.

COUNT: And you prefer him to good old reliable Coronato.

GIANNINA: I'd prefer him to others besides Coronato.

COUNT: What others?

GIANNINA: Forget I spoke.

COUNT: Look, I'm your brother's protector. Your brother has promised you to Coronato and you ought to marry Coronato.

GIANNINA: My brother has promised me to Coronato?

COUNT: He has indeed.

GIANNINA: That puts a different complexion on it.

COUNT: It does?

GIANNINA: It certainly does. If my brother has made a promise…

COUNT: Yes?

GIANNINA: Let him marry Coronato. I'm sure they'll be very happy.

COUNT: I swear you won't marry Crespino.

GIANNINA: Why not?

COUNT: I'll banish him from the village.

GIANNINA: I'll follow him.

COUNT: I'll have him horse-whipped.

GIANNINA: He's pretty handy with a whip himself.

COUNT: I'll have him killed.

GIANNINA: That would be inconvenient.

COUNT: What would you do if he was dead?

GIANNINA: How do I know? He isn't.

COUNT: Would you take someone else?

GIANNINA: Possibly.

COUNT: Count on him being dead.

GIANNINA: Sorry, your Excellency, nobody ever taught me to count. Anything else?

COUNT: You little madam!

GIANNINA: I'll be off, then.

COUNT: Yes, go to hell.

GIANNINA: I'm sure you could give me directions. 'Bye. Your Honour.

She exits.

COUNT: Damn! I can't force her to marry Coronato. What is he thinking about wanting to marry a girl who doesn't want him!

Another translation of the play is available in *Goldoni: Three Comedies* (Oxford).

THE MAGISTRATE

by Sir Arthur Wing Pinero

The Magistrate of the title, AENEAS POSKET, has recently married a widow, AGATHA. AGATHA is thirty-five but, in order to make herself seem a better 'prospect' has claimed to be thirty. This meant that she also had to lie about the age of her son, CIS. Though CIS is nineteen, he and everyone in the POSKET household believes him to be an unusually mature fourteen year old and treats him accordingly. In this, the opening scene of the play, CIS is having piano lessons from BEATIE TOMLINSON, a most attractive young woman and protegée of the Magistrate.

BEATIE is playing the piano as CIS enters.

CIS: Beatie!

BEATIE: Cis, dear. Dinner isn't over, surely?

CIS: Not quite. I had one of my convenient headaches and came out.

He takes an apple and some nuts from his pockets and gives them to her.

These are for you, dear, with all my love. I sneaked 'em off the sideboard as I came out.

BEATIE: Oh, I mustn't take them.

CIS: Yes, you may – it's my share of dessert. Besides, it's a horrid shame you don't grub with us.

BEATIE: What? A poor little music mistress?

CIS: Yes. They're only going to give you four guineas a quarter. Fancy getting a girl like you for four guineas a quarter – why, an eighth of you is worth more than that! Now, peg away at your apple.

BEATIE: There's company at dinner, isn't there?

CIS: Well, hardly. Aunt Charlotte hasn't arrived yet so there's only old Bullamy.

BEATIE: Isn't old Bullamy anybody?

CIS: Old Bullamy – well, he's only like the Guv'nor, a police magistrate at the Mulberry Street police court.

BEATIE: Oh, does each police court have two magistrates?

CIS: (*Proudly.*) All the best have two.

BEATIE: Don't they quarrel about getting the interesting cases?

CIS: I don't know how they manage – perhaps they toss up who's to hear the big sensations. There's a Mrs Beldam who's rather a bore sometimes; I know the Guv'nor lets old Bullamy attend to her. But as a rule, I fancy they go half and half, in a friendly way. For instance, if the Guv'nor wants to go to the Derby, he lets old Bullamy have the Oaks – and so on, see?

He reclines on the floor, leaning against BEATIE.

BEATIE: I say, Cis, won't your Mamma be angry when she finds I haven't gone home?

CIS: Oh, put it on your pupil. (*Looking at her winningly.*) Say I'm very backward.

BEATIE: I think you are extremely forward – in some ways. I do wish I could get you to concentrate your attention on your music lessons. But I wouldn't get you into a scrape.

CIS: No fear of that. Ma is too proud of me.

BEATIE: But there's your stepfather.

CIS: (*Laughing.*) The dear old Guv'nor. Why, he's too good-natured to say 'Boo' to a goose. You know, Beatie, I was at school in Brighton when Ma got married – when she got married the second time, I mean – and the Guv'nor and I didn't make each other's acquaintance till after the honeymoon.

BEATIE: (*Giving him a nut to crack for her.*) Fancy your stepfather blindly accepting such a responsibility.

CIS: (*Cracking nut.*) Yes, wasn't the Guv'nor soft? I might have been a very indifferent sort of fellow for all he knew.

Having cracked the nut with his teeth, he returns it to her.

BEATIE: Thank you, dear.

CIS: Well, when I heard the new dad was a police magistrate, I *was* scared. Said I to myself, 'If I don't mind my Ps and Qs, the Guv'nor – from force of habit – will fine me all my pocket money.' But it's quite the reverse – he's the mildest, meekest… Look out! Someone's coming!

They jump up and BEATIE starts to play the piano.

False alarm!

CIS has an idea. He goes to the table, pours a glass of brandy from the decanter, and takes it to BEATIE.

Here you are, Beatie, dear.

BEATIE: The idea of such a thing. I couldn't.

CIS: Why not?

BEATIE: If I merely sipped it, I shouldn't be able to give you your piano lesson properly. Drink it yourself, you dear, thoughtful boy.

CIS: I shan't. It's for you.

BEATIE: I can't drink it.

CIS: You must.

BEATIE: I won't.

CIS: You're disagreeable.

BEATIE: Not half so disagreeable as you.

CIS: I may only be fourteen, but I feel like a grown-up man. You're only sixteen, there's not much different – and if you will only wait for me, I'll soon catch you up and be as much a man as you are a woman. (*Lovingly.*) Will you wait for me, Beatie?

BEATIE: I can't. I'm getting older every minute.

CIS: Oh, I wish I could borrow five or six years from somebody.

BEATIE: Many a person would be glad to lend them. And, oh, I wish you could.

CIS: (*Putting his arm round her.*) You do? Why?

BEATIE: Because I – because I –

CIS: Look out! Here's the Mater.

They run to the piano – he resumes playing and she counts.

BEATIE: One and two – and one – and two –

Available in *Pinero: Three Plays* (Methuen).

TIMON OF ATHENS

by William Shakespeare

This is probably Shakespeare's least-performed play. It concerns the wealthy TIMON who becomes convinced of the hypocrisy and unworthiness of mankind and, in disgust, retires to a cave outside Athens where he rages against the world. In this scene he is visited by FLAVIUS, his former steward.

FLAVIUS: O you gods!
    Is yond despised and ruinous man my lord?
    Full of decay and failing? O monument
    And wonder of good deeds evilly bestow'd!
    What an alteration of honour
    Has desperate want made!
    What viler thing upon the earth than friends
    Who can bring noblest minds to basest ends.
    How rarely does it meet with this time's guise
    When man was wish'd to love his enemies.
    Grant I may ever love, and rather woo
    Those that would mischief me than those that do!
    He's caught me in his eye: I will present
    My honest grief unto him, and, as my lord,
    Still serve him with my life. My dearest master!

TIMON: Away! What art thou?

FLAVIUS: Have you forgot me, sir?

TIMON: Why dost ask that? I have forgot all men;
    Then, if thou grant'st thou'rt a man, I have forgot thee.

FLAVIUS: An honest poor servant of yours.

TIMON: Then I know thee not:
    I never had an honest man about me, I; all
    I kept were knaves, to serve in meat to villains.

FLAVIUS: The gods are witness,
    Ne'er did poor steward wear a truer grief
    For his undone lord than mine eyes for you.

TIMON: What, dost thou weep? Come nearer; then I love thee,
    Because thou art a woman, and disclaim'st
    Flinty mankind, whose eyes do never give
    But thorough lust and laughter. Pity's sleeping:
    Strange times, that weep with laughing, not with weeping.

FLAVIUS: I beg of you to know me, good my lord,
    To accept my grief, and while this poor wealth lasts
    To entertain me as your steward still.

TIMON: Had I a steward
    So true, so just, and now so comfortable?
    It almost turns my dangerous nature mild.
    Let me behold thy face. Surely this man
    Was born of woman.
    Forgive my general and exceptless rashness,
    You perpetual-sober gods! I do proclaim
    One honest man – mistake me not – but one;
    No more, I pray – and he's a steward.
    How fain I would have hated all mankind!
    And thou redeem'st thyself: but all, save thee,
    I fell with curses.
    Methinks thou art more honest now than wise;
    For, by oppressing and betraying me,
    Thou might'st have sooner got another service:
    For many so arrive at second masters,
    Upon their first lord's neck. But tell me true –
    For I must ever doubt, thou ne'er so sure –
    Is not thy kindness subtle, covetous,
    If not a usuring kindness and as rich men deal gifts,
    Expecting in return twenty for one?

FLAVIUS: No, my most worthy master; in whose breast
    Doubt and suspect, alas, are placed too late:
    You should have fear'd false times when you did feast:

Suspect still comes when an estate is least.
That which I show, heaven knows, is merely love,
Duty and zeal to your unmatched mind,
Care of your food and living; and, believe it,
My most honour'd lord,
For any benefit that points to me,
Either in hope or present, I'd exchange
For this one wish, that you had power and wealth
To requite me by making rich yourself.

TIMON: Look, thee, 'tis so! Thou singly honest man
Here, take: (*Gives money.*) the gods, out of my misery,
Have sent thee treasure. Go, live rich and happy;
But thus condition'd: thou shalt build from men,
Hate all, curse all, show charity to none,
But let the famish'd flesh slide from the bone
Ere thou relieve the beggar: give to dogs
What thou deniest to men; let prisons swallow 'em,
Debts with 'em to nothing: be men like blasted woods,
And may diseases lick up their false bloods!
And so farewell, and thrive.

FLAVIUS: O let me stay
And comfort you, my master.

TIMON: If thou had'st curses
Stay not: fly, while thou art blest and free:
Ne'er see thou man, and let me ne'er see thee.

Available in any *Complete Works* of Shakespeare or any
individual edition of *Timon of Athens.*

THE IMPORTANCE OF BEING EARNEST

by Oscar Wilde

This scene is taken from Wilde's original four act version of the play and was cut from the version which is generally performed today. JACK WORTHING lives a double life. He has a house in the country where his ward, CECILY, lives. JACK maintains the illusion that he has a disreputable younger brother, ERNEST, who lives in London. In fact, 'ERNEST' is himself. His friend, ALGERNON MONCRIEFF, has discovered JACK's trick and has arrived at the country house pretending to be 'ERNEST'. Here, a solicitor, GRIBSBY, comes to make a claim on 'ERNEST WORTHING' – a debt that JACK, of course, has run up but ALGERNON has to answer for.

GRIBSBY: Mr Ernest Worthing?

ALGERNON: Yes.

GRIBSBY: Of B4, The Albany?

ALGERNON: Yes, that is my address.

GRIBSBY: I am very sorry, sir, but we have a writ of attachment for twenty days against you at the suit of the Savoy Hotel Co. Limited for seven hundred and sixty-two pounds, fourteen shillings and twopence.

ALGERNON: Against me?

GRIBSBY: Yes, sir.

ALGERNON: What perfect nonsense! I never dine at the Savoy at my own expense. I always dine at Willis's. It is far more expensive. I don't owe a penny to the Savoy.

GRIBSBY: The writ is marked as having been served on you personally at the Albany on May the 27th. Judgement was given in default against you on the fifth of June.

Since then we have written to you no less than fifteen times without receiving any reply. In the interest of our client we had no option but to obtain an order for the committal of your person.

ALGERNON: Committal! What on earth do you mean by committal? I haven't the smallest intention of going away. I am staying here for a week. I am staying with my brother. If you imagine I am going up to town the moment I arrive you are extremely mistaken.

GRIBSBY: I am merely a solicitor myself. I do not employ personal violence of any kind. The Officer of the Court, whose function it is to seize the person of the debtor, is waiting in the fly outside. He has considerable experience of these matters. That is why we always employ him. But no doubt you will prefer to pay the bill.

ALGERNON: Pay it? How on earth am I going to do that? You don't suppose I have got any money? How perfectly silly you are. No gentleman ever has any money.

GRIBSBY: My experience is that it is usually relations who pay.

ALGERNON: Jack, you really must settle this bill. You know perfectly well the bill is really yours. You know it is.

GRIBSBY: I am sorry to disturb this pleasant family meeting, but time presses. We have to be at Holloway no later than four o'clock; otherwise it is difficult to obtain admission. The rules are very strict.

ALGERNON: Holloway!

GRIBSBY: It is at Holloway that detentions of this character take place always.

ALGERNON: Well, I really am not going to be imprisoned in the suburbs for having dined in the West End.

GRIBSBY: The bill is for suppers, not dinners.

ALGERNON: I really don't care. All I say is that I am not going to be imprisoned in the suburbs.

GRIBSBY: The surroundings, I admit, are middle-class; but the gaol itself is fashionable and well-aired; and there are ample opportunities of taking exercise at certain stated hours of the day. In the case of a medical certificate, which is always easy to obtain, the hours can be extended.

ALGERNON: Exercise! Good God! No gentleman ever takes exercise. You don't seem to understand what a gentleman is.

GRIBSBY: I have met so many of them, sir, that I am afraid I don't. There are the most curious varieties of them. The result of cultivation, no doubt. Will you kindly come now, sir, if it will not be inconvenient to you?

ALGERNON: Jack… Oh, thank Heavens.

GRIBSBY: (*To JACK.*) I will certainly take your cheque, sir. Seven hundred and sixty-two pounds, fourteen shillings and twopence. Ah! The cab will be five-and-ninepence extra: hired for the convenience of the client. Payable to Parker and Gribsby. Kindly don't cross the cheque. Thank you. (*To ALGERNON.*) Good day, sir. I hope I shall have the pleasure of meeting you again.

ALGERNON: I sincerely hope not. What ideas you have of the sort of society a gentleman wants to mix in. No gentleman ever wants to know a solicitor who wants to imprison one in the suburbs.

GRIBSBY: Quite so, quite so.

ALGERNON: By the way, Gribsby: Gribsby, you are not to go back to the station in that cab. That is my cab. It was taken for my convenience. You have got to walk to the station. And a very good thing, too. Solicitors don't walk nearly enough. I don't know any solicitor who takes sufficient exercise. As a rule they sit in stuffy offices all day long neglecting their business.

GRIBSBY: Thank you, sir.

GRIBSBY exits. ALGERNON rubs his hands together.

ALGERNON: Lunch, I think. I am excessively hungry.

Available in *The Complete Works of Oscar Wilde* (Collins).

SHE STOOPS TO CONQUER

by Oliver Goldsmith

MARLOW and HASTINGS are two young gentlemen who believe themselves to be lodged in an inn – in fact, they are in the home of SQUIRE HARDCASTLE. In this scene, they have just been shown into the parlour and are making themselves comfortable.

HASTINGS: After the disappointments of the day, welcome once more, Charles, to the comforts of a clean room and a good fire. Upon my word, a very well-looking house; antique, but creditable.

MARLOW: The usual fate of a large mansion. Having first ruined the master by good housekeeping, it at last comes to levy contributions as an inn!

HASTINGS: As you say, we passengers are to be taxed to pay all these fineries. I have often seen a good sideboard, or a marble chimney-piece, tho' not actually put in the bill, enflame a reckoning confoundedly.

MARLOW: Travellers, George, must pay in all places. The only difference is, that in good inns, you pay dearly for luxuries; in bad inns, you are fleeced and starved.

HASTINGS: You have lived pretty much among them. In truth, I have been often surprised, that you have seen so much of the world, with your natural good sense, and your many opportunities, could never yet acquire a requisite share of assurance.

MARLOW: The Englishman's malady. But tell me, George, where could I have learned that assurance you talk of? My life has been chiefly spent in a college, or an inn, in seclusion from that lovely part of the creation that chiefly teach men confidence. I don't know that I was ever familiarly acquainted with a single modest woman – except my mother – But among females of another class, you know –

HASTINGS: Ay, among them you are impudent enough of all conscience.

MARLOW: They are of *us* you know.

HASTINGS: But in the company of women of reputation I never saw such an idiot, such a trembler; you look for all the world as if you wanted an opportunity of stealing out of the room.

MARLOW: Why, man, that's because I *do* want to steal out of the room. Faith, I have often formed a resolution to break the ice, and rattle away at any rate. But I don't know how, a single glance from a pair of fine eyes has totally overset my resolution. An impudent fellow may counterfeit modesty, but I'll be hanged if a modest man can ever counterfeit impudence.

HASTINGS: If you could but say half the fine things to them that I have heard you lavish upon the bar-maid of an inn, or even a college bed maker –

MARLOW: Why, George, I can't say fine things to them. They freeze, they petrify me. They may talk of a comet, or a burning mountain, or some such bagatelle. But to me, a modest woman, dressed out in all her finery, is the most tremendous object of the whole creation.

HASTINGS: (*Laughs.*) At this rate, man, how can you ever expect to marry?

MARLOW: Never, unless as among kings and princes, my bride were to be courted by proxy. If, indeed, like an Eastern bridegroom, one were to be introduced to a wife he never saw before, it might be endured. But to go through all the terrors of a formal courtship, together with the episode of aunts, grandmothers and cousins, and at last to blurt out the broad staring question, of 'Madam, will you marry me…' No, no, that's a strain much above me I assure you.

HASTINGS: I pity you. But how do you intend behaving to the lady you are come down to visit at the request of your father ?

MARLOW: As I behave to all other ladies. Bow very low. Answer yes, or no, to all her demands – But for the rest, I don't think I shall venture to look in her face, till I see my father's again.

HASTINGS: I'm surprised that one who is so warm a friend can be so cool a lover.

MARLOW: To be explicit, my dear Hastings, my chief inducement down was to be instrumental in forwarding your happiness, not my own. Miss Neville loves you, the family don't know you, as my friend you are sure of a reception, and let honour do the rest.

HASTINGS: My dear Marlow! But I'll suppress the emotion. Were I a wretch, meanly seeking to carry off a fortune, you should be the last man in the world I would apply to for assistance. But Miss Neville's person is all I ask, and that is mine, both from her deceased father's consent, and her own inclination.

MARLOW: Happy man! You have talents and art to captivate any woman. I'm doom'd to adore the sex, and yet to converse with the only part of it I despise. This stammer in my address, and this awkward, unprepossessing visage of mine, can never permit me to soar above the reach of a milliner's apprentice, or one of the duchesses of Drury Lane. (*Hearing a noise, off.*) Pshaw! this fellow is here to interrupt us.

Available in *Eighteenth Century Comedy* (Oxford).

AFTER DARK

by Dion Boucicault

CHANDOS BELLINGHAM is an unscrupulous fugitive from justice who is blackmailing SIR GEORGE MEDHURST. Here, BELLINGHAM has come to make financial arrangements and is expecting to meet his victim. Instead, MEDHURST is represented by SIR GORDON CHUMLEY, an honourable Captain of Dragoons.

CHUMLEY: Good day, sir.

BELLINGHAM: I expected to see Sir George Medhurst.

CHUMLEY: I know it. But you see me instead.

BELLINGHAM: It was a private matter – and important.

CHUMLEY: I know that, too, but I still believe Sir George will not lose by my intermediation.

BELLINGHAM: I should say not.

CHUMLEY: I act just as if it were himself. Can you spare me five minutes?

BELLINGHAM: Five minutes? No more, for I must catch the train that leaves for town in ten minutes.

CHUMLEY: I will be as brief as I can. Sir George has told me by what means he is in the power of Mrs Morris and yourself.

BELLINGHAM: The more fool he.

CHUMLEY: Perhaps we shall alter our opinion on that point before our conversation is finished.

BELLINGHAM: You know the terms?

CHUMLEY: Yes, but we will pay only double what is on the face of the note.

BELLINGHAM: Mrs Morris would never listen to such a proposition.

CHUMLEY: Then Mrs Morris mistakes the value of the paper. I rely upon you to undeceive her.

BELLINGHAM: Upon me? Your confidence does me honour.

CHUMLEY: You flatter me.

BELLINGHAM: Not at all. I'll listen to you.

CHUMLEY: I do not forget your perspicacity as shown on other occasions.

BELLINGHAM: On 'other occasions'. I beg your pardon?

CHUMLEY: Yes. Seven years ago I was stationed at Melbourne. I was ordered out to assist the constabulary in the arrest of a notorious bushranger, one Richard Knatchbull.

BELLINGHAM: *Richard* Knatchbull. Ah! And you – ah – caught him?

CHUMLEY: Yes, we caught him. And while we held him in custody, curiosity impelled me to inspect this 'wild beast'.

BELLINGHAM: And I suppose you think him like me?

CHUMLEY: Yes, very like you. The first time I met you since, at the railway, I recognised –

BELLINGHAM: His features on my face. Ah, poor Dick. My elder brother, sir. He has been my ruin. His reputation has blasted mine and caused me to live under a false name. So you caught him? You hanged him, of course?

CHUMLEY: No, he escaped.

BELLINGHAM: Did he indeed? Ah, he has as many lives as a cat.

CHUMLEY: I beg your pardon, Mr Bellingham, I really thought that you were the fellow and meant to use that as a weapon against you.

BELLINGHAM: I saw you did. But never mind apologies. It is my misfortune, not your fault.

CHUMLEY: I am very sorry that you are not the other scoundrel.

BELLINGHAM: Don't mention it.

CHUMLEY: But to business. Sir George will give five thousand pounds to be released.

BELLINGHAM: My partner would never think of such an idea.

CHUMLEY: Six thousand?

BELLINGHAM: It is hopeless.

CHUMLEY: Eight thousand?

BELLINGHAM: It is useless to mention it.

CHUMLEY: As a last sum, ten thousand?

BELLINGHAM: You are losing time and I shall miss the train. I have but five minutes to reach the station.

CHUMLEY: (*His watch out.*) You have lost it. Your watch has stopped.

BELLINGHAM: (*Puts watch to right ear.*) No.

CHUMLEY: Why do you test it by your right ear? Because Richard Knatchbull lost his left ear at Harper's Ferry.

BELLINGHAM: Checkmate! The game is yours. You have mistaken your profession.

CHUMLEY: I am a soldier.

BELLINGHAM: Nature has richly endowed you for the profession of detective. Well, I think you mentioned ten thousand pounds?

CHUMLEY: Sir George would never think of such an idea.

BELLINGHAM: Eight thousand?

CHUMLEY: It is useless to mention it.

BELLINGHAM: Six thousand?

CHUMLEY: Quite hopeless, I assure you.

BELLINGHAM: Then what are your terms?

CHUMLEY: Double that on the face of the note.

BELLINGHAM: If I accept it, you will make no use of the secret in your hands?

CHUMLEY: Safety for safety! When and where shall I have the pleasure to see you?

BELLINGHAM: At the Silver Bell, in the Broadway, Westminster, tonight.

CHUMLEY: I will come.

They exit, separately.

Available in *Melodrama Classics*, edited by Dorothy Mackin (Sterling Publishing Co).

Also published by Oberon Books in association with LAMDA:

Solo Speeches for Men (1800-1914)
ISBN: 1 84002 046 6

Solo Speeches for Women (1800-1914)
ISBN:1 84002 003 2

The LAMDA Anthology of Verse and Prose, Vol XV
ISBN: 1 84002 120 9

The LAMDA Guide to English Literature
ISBN: 1 84002 011 3

Scenes for Teenagers
ISBN: 1 84002 031 8

Solo Speeches for Under-12s
ISBN: 1 84002 013 X

Meaning, Form and Performance
ISBN: 1 870259 74 2

First Folio Speeches for Men
ISBN: 1 84002 015 6

First Folio Speeches for Women
ISBN: 1 84002 014 8

Contemporary Scenes for Young Women (1985-2000)
ISBN: 1 84002 130 6

Contemporary Scenes for Young Men (1985-2000)
ISBN: 1 84002 141 1

The Discussion (2nd edition)
ISBN: 1 870259 71 8

Mime and Improvisation
ISBN: 1 84002 012 1